the SHOT caller SERIES

OK, i will

WATCHING GOD'S HAND MOVE

Casey Diaz

with MIKE YORKEY

To Mickey Dysthe

who has and continues
to keep everything flowing . . .

TABLE OF CONTENTS

A NOTE FROM CASEY DIAZ

Since the release of *The Shot Caller* in the spring of 2019, I've heard from countless people impacted by my story as a hardened gang leader who relished meting out violence on others until Jesus met me in solitary lockup. They said my memoir pulled no punches and called it a "bare-knuckle read" of a young man—a teenager, actually—who sought affirmation from the street thugs who jumped me into their gang in downtown Los Angeles.

While the readers' comments meant a great deal, hearing how *The Shot Caller* changed lives in the prison system bolstered me the most. I received emails and phone calls from wardens, prison chaplains, and COs (correctional officers) who said my story either changed the culture in certain cell blocks or dozens of prisoners were prompted to get right with the Lord and start attending chapel.

And then there were the handwritten letters from the prisoners themselves—murderers, thieves, and sex offenders, some serving life sentences—who told me they couldn't put *The Shot Caller* down, and what I had to say resonated with them. They said I gave them hope, an emotion in short supply inside prison walls.

What you're about to read are inspiring and informative stories that have—to use a modern term—six degrees of separation from *The Shot Caller*. Not only will you hear from prison authorities, inmates, and ex-cons, but you'll also read stories from people outside the penal system that will blow your mind. In a few places, I'll make some comments.

But in case you don't know my background, or it's been a few years since you read *The Shot Caller*, let me offer you a refresher of a story I love sharing with audiences and anyone who will listen.

✦ ✦ ✦

What is a "shot caller"?

The term "shot caller" refers to gang leaders with an elevated rank in the gang world. Not only do we command respect, but we are power brokers inside prison walls and determine who gets hurt (or killed) and who doesn't.

Shot callers have street cred, which I had in spades as one of the leaders of the Rockwood Street Locos in South-Central Los Angeles. I led the way when we did home invasions, carried out car break-ins, ransacked convenience stores, and conducted another round of tit-for-tat stabbings of rival gang members. It didn't take me long to figure out that the streets were bloody. Most of the time, it was kill or be killed.

Eventually, I was caught by the LAPD and got tagged with a murder rap. The Los Angeles Superior Court sentenced me to a twelve-year, eight-month term for second-degree murder and *fifty-two* counts of armed robbery. I breathed a sigh of relief that those were the only charges the cops could pin on me.

While awaiting transfer to New Folsom State Prison—a Level IV maximum security prison near Sacramento, California—I was housed with 120 murderers and violent criminals in the 2400 East Max wing inside Pitchess Detention Center, north of Los Angeles.

At Pitchess, we segregated ourselves: blacks aligning with blacks, whites aligning with whites, and browns—the Latinos—aligning with browns. Several dudes from two long-established gangs—18th Street and Florencia 13—approached me and asked me to become a "shot caller" inside 2400 East Max.

One of the shot callers' responsibilities was to control the shanks within the prison population—the crude homemade knives used for stabbing another prisoner. I became the one who slept with the shanks—all thirteen of them under my mattress. You may be wondering: *If I'm part of your gang, why would I give* you *my shank? Why give up that power?*

Here's my answer: when you're appointed to be a shot caller, it would be suicidal not to give me your shank because if you don't, you're done. I'll have you killed.

There were many violent upheavals at Pitchess, and inmates were stabbed and killed all the time. When a riot went off, I made sure the right people had the killing weapons. All it took was one wrong look at the wrong person, and you were done for.

Life was very cheap.

✦　✦　✦

After six months, I was transferred to New Folsom State Prison, a sprawling correctional facility surrounded by smooth concrete walls three stories high. When the prison bus dropped us off at the main building, I saw guards pacing on catwalks, their arms cradling Mini-14s—small, lightweight, semi-automatic rifles.

Standing next to a phalanx of serious-looking guards dressed in riot gear, the warden cleared his throat. "I want you to look at the sign to your right."

My eyes alighted on a white sign with red lettering:

No Warning Shots Fired

"You'll notice that there will be absolutely no warning shots fired by my guards. In case of a riot, we will not be aiming at your feet, we will not be aiming at your legs, and we will not be aiming at your torso. We will be aiming directly at your head to kill you."

With the end of that cheery pep talk, the warden issued a chipper "Welcome, and enjoy your stay" salutation, turned on his heels, and left the yard.

When the warden was gone, a guard approached me with a manila file in his right hand. "Diaz, follow me," he ordered.

I was led inside the prison to an interview room, where the guard introduced himself as a gang coordinator.

"Listen closely, Diaz. We know you're a banger and a shot caller, so we're putting you in SHU, in solitary."

Security Housing Units (SHU, which is pronounced *shoe*) were the most secure areas within the prison and prison shorthand for solitary confinement. I would *not* be sharing a cell with one, two, or three other prisoners, nor would I be housed in a dorm-style environment like I was at Pitchess. Instead, I would be cooped up in an eight-by-ten-foot windowless cell. I would eat all my meals inside my cell with my food slipped through a slot in the steel door, or "gate." Social interactions with other inmates would be nonexistent or severely limited at best. Ditto for the guards.

Since I had no windows and thus no daylight, my tiny cell was dimly illuminated by a heavy Plexiglas light in the ceiling that couldn't be turned off. This meant I had to sleep—or at least try to—with a light on the entire time. Further compounding my disorientation was having no clock or wristwatch inside the cell, which meant that I had trouble distinguishing whether it was day or night or what time it was. Only the arrival of my meals around 5 a.m., 11 a.m., and 5 p.m. gave me any sense of what time it could be.

There wasn't anything inside my prison cell—no TV, no radio, and no books because I was denied this privilege. Add this all up, and it meant that I had nothing to do for twenty-three hours a day.

There were times when I wondered if I could keep my sanity. Prisoners in Pitchess told me that if you're not strong-minded and strong-willed, solitary confinement could totally break you.

I quickly realized why they said that.

✦ ✦ ✦

After a year or so at New Folsom, I heard the guards come by my cell with an announcement: "Protestant service. Any inmate wanting to go, stand by your gate."

I had heard the same announcement for Catholics. Religion wasn't something I was interested in. I knew next to nothing about God or Jesus Christ except that he was the one who was on all those crucifixes. I wasn't sure why that happened, but I didn't care.

One time, I was lying on my bed, listening to the voices outside. I heard an older woman say, "Is someone in that cell?" She sounded Southern and spoke with a syrupy drawl.

"Yes, ma'am, but you don't want to deal with Diaz," the guard said. "You're wasting your time."

"Well, Jesus came for him, too."

She approached the cell. "Young man, can I speak with you?"

I looked through the open slot in my gate. I couldn't see anything except for the guard's boots and a pair of spindly legs. Her skin tone confirmed the accent in her voice: she was African American.

"How are you doing?" she asked.

"I couldn't be better," I replied with plenty of sarcasm.

"Young man, I'm going to pray for you. But there's something else I want to tell you: Jesus is going to use you."

That statement confirmed that this lady was crazy. Couldn't she see that I had been thrown into solitary confinement with the lock and key thrown away? And she thought Jesus was going to use me?

"I don't think that's going to happen," I said.

"Young man, every time I'm here, I'm going to come by and remind you that Jesus is going to use you."

A year or so later, I was lying down in my cell. I was daydreaming when I turned my head toward the wall opposite my bed.

On that wall, a movie was playing—a film about my life. I saw myself as a young child, walking the old neighborhood at 9th and Kenmore. I witnessed incidents from the schoolyard and my early days with the gang—everything was in picture-perfect detail. There were scenes that only I would know and remember. This movie of my life was displayed on my cell wall in vivid color like there was a movie projector next to my bed.

This was weird. Really weird. I was wide awake, but what I was seeing was my entire life story from when I was a young child—in a film.

Then I saw a bearded man with long hair carrying a cross. A mob of angry people shouted at this man as he shuffled along with a cross over his shoulder. When he arrived on top of a knoll, rough-looking men nailed his hands and feet to the wooden beams and raised the cross so it stood between two men, each affixed to their own crosses.

I didn't understand what was going on. All I knew was that I must be going nuts. What got to me was when this person being crucified looked at me and said, "Darwin, I'm doing this for you."

I shuddered. No one knew my real name. Of course, the guards knew and so did my family, but nobody at New Folsom called me by my given name. Everyone called me Casey—a nickname I'd had as long as I could remember. Yet this man on a cross said, "Darwin, I'm doing this for you."

And then I heard the sound of breath leaving him. At that moment, I knew he had died.

That's when I hit the floor in the middle of the cell. I started weeping because I knew somehow that this was Almighty God, even though I didn't understand what he had done for me or what was happening.

After hitting the floor, I knew I had to get on my knees. I started confessing my sins.

God, I'm sorry for stabbing so many people.
God, I'm sorry I robbed so many families.
God, I'm sorry for stabbing that gang member in the eye.

Each time I confessed something I had done, I felt like another weight came off my shoulders. When I finished, I knew something significant had definitely happened.

I asked to see a chaplain, who opened his Bible and explained who Jesus was. He told me that what I experienced in my cell was salvation. When our meeting was over, he handed me a Bible and urged me to start reading, which I did.

I'd spend five or six hours reading that Bible, then fall asleep, wake up, do some push-ups and calisthenics, and get back to reading from where I left off. I didn't understand half of what I was reading, but that didn't even bother me.

That was the start of my journey of faith. I was eventually released from the SHU and sent into the mainline prison population, where I was beaten for being a Christian and turning my back on my fellow gang members, but I was okay with that.

I was no longer a shot caller, but I had found a new calling—telling other inmates about Jesus.

Then another miracle happened several years later: I was released from prison early and returned to Los Angeles, where I became a part-time pastor while owning a sign-making business. Every now and then, I'd speak to groups or share my story with individuals, including an acquaintance named Mical Pyeatt. He was so blown away that he said that he wanted to help me get my story into a book and possibly become a movie. More on all that later.

There's a lot to talk about, but I feel the urgency to get moving. I'll start by sharing how I realized something special was happening when *The Shot Caller* book was released a few years ago. Then you'll hear from Mical Pyeatt and others.

As you read through the pages of *Ok, I Will*, keep this thought in mind: at one time, I marked people for death.

Then Jesus marked me for life.

part
1

THE STORY
BEHIND THE STORY

chapter one

GETTING MY WINGS

A lot of people don't remember their first plane flight.
That's because they were very young—just a few months or a few years old—when their mothers wheeled them down a Jetway, or they walked aboard an airliner holding the hand of an older sibling for their first time in the air.

But I certainly remember my first flight and can even recall the date: March 31, 2019. I was forty-six years old, which may sound ancient but not where I'm from—the Rampart District of downtown Los Angeles.

Anyone growing up in neighborhoods like MacArthur Park, Pico-Union, Koreatown, Watts, Compton, or South-Central shared something in common: we never stepped outside a four-mile radius from our home. None of us even visited the beach, even though the Santa Monica Pier and its wide, sandy shoreline was only fifteen miles away, no more than a thirty-minute drive west on Interstate 10.

But living in Rampart, you never go outside your pocket. You stuck with what you knew, even if you had money to burn. That was my world growing up—a world of mean, unforgiving streets in which rival gangs marked their territory and protected their criminal activities through violence and intimidation.

I was boarding my first flight on a sunny Sunday morning because my book, *The Shot Caller*, was due to be released two days later on April 2, 2019. Eminate, the book publisher and an imprint of HarperCollins, had lined up a bunch of interviews and appearances in Washington, D.C., and New York City, and they were paying the freight.

Joining me was Mical Pyeatt, a special friend who'd been trying to help me tell my story for seven years. (You'll learn more about Mical in the next chapter.) The plan called for us to fly to Dallas, where we'd meet up with Joel Kneedler, the publisher of Emanate Books, for the final leg to Washington, D.C.

So, imagine my excitement when my wife, Sana, dropped Mical and me off at the Hollywood Burbank Airport, one of Los Angeles' five regional airports only ten minutes from our home in Burbank. I wanted Sana to come with me, but we had three school-age children to look after. She planted a kiss on my cheek and wished us a safe trip.

Once Sana left the curb, everything was new to me—the hustle and bustle of people moving about, finding the right place to check in, handing over my suitcase, and watching the lady behind the counter heft the travel bag onto her leg and dump it on a black conveyor belt.

"You'll find security on your right," the female check-in agent said as she handed me my boarding pass and baggage claim ticket.

I followed Mical's lead as we left the counter. I could tell this check-in business seemed as natural as buttering a slice of toast to him.

"What did she mean by security?" I asked as we made our way to the gate.

"The government set up a system where they check passengers for any guns or knives before they board a plane," he explained. "It's called TSA."

There was a time when I didn't travel anywhere without a gun, a knife, or a screwdriver that I used in lethal ways, but those days were long past. As for going through a scanner and getting patted down? I could do that. I had lots of practice at the LA County Jail.

Sure enough, I knew exactly what to do when going through security. Mical and I made our way to the gate and found seats in the lounge, which was filling up with families and other passengers.

"Here's what's going to happen," Mical said. "Southwest doesn't give out seat assignments like the other airlines, so we have to board by zone. When we walk on, we can sit wherever we want."

"Got it," I replied, getting more excited by the minute.

Mical let me walk down the Jetway first. When I stepped onto the plane, I couldn't get over how long the interior seating was.[1] I led the way down the aisle, squeezing past people lifting their carry-on baggage into the bins above the seats. Then I saw a near-empty row on the left: a woman was already seated next to the window, leaving two empty seats.

"Looks good to me," I said to Mical as I settled into the middle seat. I thought I chose the perfect row and the perfect seat: I could look out through the side window throughout the flight, and my buddy could sit next to me on the aisle, his favorite place to sit, he told me. Middle seats were the best seats, I decided.

The commotion caused by the boarding of the last passengers fascinated me. Some were taking their time when I heard an announcement over the PA system: "People, we're not picking out furniture here. Please find a seat and get in it so we can have an on-time departure."

Mical chuckled. "Southwest is the only airline that doesn't assign seats," he said. "They also don't have first class."

"What's first class?"

Mical smiled. "I'll tell you another time."

After the final groups of passengers filed past to the rear of the plane, there was another series of announcements from a male Southwest flight

---

1 I wasn't aware that Southwest only flew single-aisle Boeing 737s with 143 or 175 seats.

attendant. The guy sounded like he was trying out for the Comedy Club.

"The weather in Dallas is 50 degrees with some broken clouds, but we'll try to have them fixed before we arrive. To operate your seat belt, insert the metal tab into the buckle and pull tight. If you don't know how to do that, you probably shouldn't be out in public unsupervised. Thank you for choosing to fly with us today, and remember, nobody loves you, or your money, more than Southwest Airlines."

When the plane backed out of the gate, I was so excited. I'm a sign guy, so being high off the ground has always been my thing. I have zero fear of heights and love installing signs seventy, one hundred feet up in the air, perched in a basket extended from a bucket truck. Now I was going to be *way* up there.

I fixed my eyes on the window as the engines roared to life, emitting a high-pitched whine. I was fascinated as the plane rolled down the runway and suddenly lifted off the ground, giving me a bird's view of the San Fernando Valley—its layout of tract homes with backyard pools and congested freeways coming into sharp relief.

I turned to Mical, who said, "Having fun yet?"

"Sure am." I felt like a kid given the run of the Disneyland candy shop on Main Street.

I turned toward the window and noticed we had climbed *way* above the ground, which was disappearing underneath us.

Twenty minutes passed when I saw a cart coming down the aisle, flanked by two female flight attendants.

"Beverage cart," Mical explained.

I was transfixed as the flight attendants poured coffee and handed out cups of water, soft drinks, and snacks.

"What would you like to drink?" asked a flight attendant as she handed me a bag of Ritz Bits crackers *and* a four-pack of Oreo cookies, my favorite. This flight just got a lot better.

"A Coke, please." My mother had taught me my manners.

I looked at Mical. "Do they always do this?" I asked.

"Every flight," he said between mouthfuls.

I was like a little kid. Wow, free snacks! No wonder people want to fly so much!

✦　✦　✦

A couple of hours into the flight, I was snoozing when Mical jostled me with his elbow.

"Look, the captain's coming our way."

"Shouldn't he be flying the plane?"

"They have two pilots on board."

"Oh."

The airline captain, wearing a white dress shirt with shoulder epaulets, a striped tie, and a military-looking cap, was saying hello to passengers as he made his way down the aisle.

When he reached our row, he stopped and looked me in the eye.

"Hello, sir. I understand this is your first time on an airplane," he said in a voice loud enough to cause everyone in the vicinity to turn around and stare at me. I noticed Mical had his head down, doing his best not to bust a gut.

"Yup. First flight."

"Then congratulations are in order. It's customary for us to award a set of wings to commemorate this milestone, so welcome aboard on behalf of Southwest Airlines. You can wear these with pride."

With that, the captain handed me a set of plastic wings, two inches wide, with a metal pin.

I noticed people chuckling out of the corner of my eye, and I knew why: I was a grown man receiving a pair of kiddie wings. I wanted to sink into my seat and disappear.

"You gotta wear your wings," Mical said.

"I do?"

"Of course."

I decided to have some fun with it, beaming as Mical pinned them on my left shirt pocket, right above my heart.

I smiled back at the other passengers looking in my direction, although I spotted a few smirks.

✦   ✦   ✦

Landing in Dallas was a trip. I'd heard everything was big in Texas, and this airport didn't disappoint.[2]

I had a text message from Joel Kneedler saying that he was waiting for us at a coffee shop near Gate 14, so that's where we headed. We had around an hour to kill before our next flight to Washington, D.C.

Mical told Joel about how I got a set of wings from the pilot, and the two of them had some fun at my expense. But then I had a question: "Wait a minute. They gotta unload our baggage. Do we have to go get it somewhere?"

"No, we don't have to do anything," Joel said. "The baggage will get to us in Washington. Most of the time, anyway."

"But how does that all work?" I didn't understand how this was possible.

"It just works somehow," Joel replied, loving every minute of this conversation.

When it came time to board, I was ready to sit in the middle seat again, but Joel insisted I take the window seat. We swooped into Washington in the evening, and my eyes were like saucers on the twenty-minute drive from the airport to our downtown hotel.[3]

Crossing the Potomac River. Driving past imposing museums. Spotting the dome of the U.S. Capitol a few streets over. The Washington Monument. The White House! It was like I was living in a fairytale.

We checked in at a nice downtown Hilton, a huge step up from

---

2 All Southwest flights land at Love Field, closer to downtown. I wasn't aware that Dallas had an even bigger airport further east that it shared with its sister city, Fort Worth, and was called DFW.

3 Though I didn't know it at the time, we landed at Reagan National Airport, just five miles from the White House and the U.S. Capitol. And yes, our luggage did arrive at the baggage carousel.

the Super 8 motels I was used to. At dinner, Joel explained that their PR crew had lined up more than a dozen interviews and probably fifteen or twenty the following day.

After the last bite of dessert, I was exhausted when I entered my room—but excited to hit the ground running in the morning.

✦ ✦ ✦

The alarm startled me at 5 a.m., which really was two o'clock in the morning back home. Mical had said I might have jet lag after we arrived. I wasn't sure what that meant, but I knew now.

My throat was sore. I tried to say something when I looked in the bathroom mirror, but my voice sounded hoarse—like a rusty gate swinging in the breeze.

Great. You're going to have to plow through it, man.

I had zero coaching on how to conduct myself in interviews. I figured being myself would be the best way to go.

We hit the ground running around 6:30 a.m. Joel seemed to know where he was going as we visited a handful of radio and TV stations throughout the morning. My interviews—generally about five to eight minutes on the radio and two or three minutes on TV—passed quickly. Some interviews were in-person in the studios, but several took place while we were driving around in the car with me in the back seat, phone glued to my ear. My head was spinning, trying to keep up.

In the late morning, I was aware that I had my biggest interview on a podcast hosted by Laura Ingraham, better known as the host of *The Ingraham Angle*, a news-and-opinion show seen on the Fox News Channel at 10 p.m. EST, but easy for me to catch since it aired at 7 o'clock in the Pacific time zone. I had listened to her long-running radio talk show a bit over the years, but she had stopped doing her syndicated, three-hour radio show a few months earlier to start her own Monday-through-Friday podcast.[4]

This was a phone-in interview, so I sat in the back of the town car until she introduced me to her audience. When I heard Laura's recognizable voice, she was curious about how I got into the gang lifestyle. "For those of us who want an inside view of how a gang operates and what it's really about, you are the perfect person to reveal that to us, so tell us," she said.

She teed up a good opening question, so I proceeded to tell her how I grew up with an alcoholic father who verbally and physically abused my mother, who worked as a seamstress, often from early in the morning until 10 p.m., to keep food on the table and a roof over our heads. Not having my parents around left me vulnerable to the streets. A gang leader took me under his wing, leading me to join his gang when I was eleven years old, which seemed to surprise Laura.

We had a pleasant conversation as she asked me more "What happened next?" questions. For ten minutes, I gave her and her listeners a stripped-down version of the story I told in *The Shot Caller*. And then she threw me a curveball.

"What are your thoughts on the issue at the border right now? I know it's not the subject of your book, but we're finding that MS-13 [one of the most notorious gangs based in Los Angeles] has brought in a significant number of people across the border, which has added difficulty in dealing with the gangs we already have in the United States. Of course, MS-13 is the worst of the worst. Any thoughts on that?"

Large caravans of migrants were traveling through Mexico in the spring of 2019, putting pressure on the border.

"Look, I understand why people are coming here for a better opportunity, to seek a dream, but there's a right way and a wrong way of doing this," I replied. "Not everyone in these caravans is coming

---

4 Laura was the most listened-to woman in talk radio before making the move to podcasting. She did so for the right reasons: the grind of a late-night TV show on Fox and a morning radio show took a toll on her and her family.

here to pick our apples. That's the bottom line. That's the truth. And there's a lot of gang activity hidden within these caravans. The reason I know that is because I was in meetings before my conversion where we discussed movements of large amounts of drugs and things like that. So, when these gang members are coming in here, they have a plan in mind, and that plan is to cause chaos.

"They're not moving into your neighborhood. They're moving into low-income housing, and their plan is to engage with young eleven-year-olds like I was. They're going to recruit from middle school all the way to high school. And by that time, we've lost a handful of American lives. We need to close the border, period. It's that serious."

Laura didn't follow up but instead had a new question for me. "Casey, are you in LA?"

"Yes."

"Next time I'm out there, let's get together and have a meal and talk. Would you like to do that? I wanna meet your family."

"I would love to do that."

"Casey, I love the book and how you turned a life of depravity, crime, and killing into a life where you're shedding light. This is why we're Christians. This is why we believe. Because as the song goes, I once was lost, but now I'm found. And I love this book. I love the fact that you're speaking out and keep doing it. And we'll see you out in LA, okay?"

I smiled and thanked Laura for the opportunity to be on the show. I was impressed with how she made me feel very comfortable—like I was sitting around her kitchen table, having coffee and just talking. But I didn't have time to dwell on those thoughts because we had to hustle to the next interview.

I'd say an hour passed when Joel got a phone call from one of the producers of *The Ingraham Angle*—her Fox TV show with more than 2.5 million nightly viewers.

"Laura loved Casey. She wants to have him in studio for tonight's show. Can you guys make it?"

This wasn't on the schedule. We were supposed to fly to New York City that evening so I could be on the "Fox & Friends" set at 6 a.m., which would set off another long day of media opportunities in the Big Apple. If we said yes to Laura, we'd have to cancel or rebook a ton of media interviews that had been set up for weeks. One of them was with Christiane Amanpour, the chief international anchor for CNN and host of *Amanpour*, a nightly interview program. That was going to be our big national TV hit—until Laura Ingraham's producer called.

Since the invitation was too good to pass up, an audible was called: we said yes to Laura Ingraham because we could reach a couple of million viewers on an influential show and expose *The Shot Caller* to a broader audience.

At the Fox studio in downtown Washington that evening, I had my first "green room" experience, waiting to go on national TV. As I munched on some snacks, I'll admit some nerves were in play.

Joel looked at me, serious. "She's going to want to talk to you about the border situation," Joel said. "You okay with that?"

"Joel, I gotta be me, man. I can't be someone else. That's just not how I do things. I gonna answer from my convictions."

I understood Laura wasn't having me on her show to talk about my book or my story, but she wanted a former LA gang leader to give his take on the border situation, which was in the news. I was also aware that guests on cable news "opinion shows" usually got two, three, or four minutes max during a segment. That's what viewers were used to.

During a commercial break, at 10:32 p.m., a producer led me to a seat opposite her on the set. Behind her was a window—with the brightly lit U.S. Capitol in the background. Now *that* surprised me. I always thought that was a picture of the Capitol behind her, but we overlooked the real deal.

But I didn't have time to get comfortable. We were live.[5]

---

5 My interview with Laura has been edited for length.

Laura Ingraham:

My next guest, Casey Diaz, is a former gang member, author of the brand-new book, *The Shot Caller*, and he has an eye-opening perspective on the dangers of open borders.

What is your message, Casey? I had you on the podcast today. You had the most unbelievable story of redemption, of juvenile crime, gangbangers, murder, and now you're out, and you're seeing this conversation about an open border. When you were on the streets dealing with the rival gangs—yours was MS-13. They were princes, I'm sure.

Casey:

You know, it's a real, actual problem that we're having, and it can't be overlooked. It needs to be tackled right now . . . and if need be, to lock it down. We see that people with good hearts want to come in here and pursue a dream. But in these caravans, I can tell you from being in meetings in the past when I was active in the gang leadership, that there were plans, there was an agenda, and in these caravans, you're going to see a lot of MS-13, a lot of 18th Street gang guys, you're going to see a lot of gangs. They're going to be dressed very normal, and they're going to try to get in here. That's just the bottom line.

Laura Ingraham:

And you write about this in your book, and it's chilling, but the means and the methods of terrorizing the most vulnerable people on the streets, and oftentimes they are the Latino Americans who are legal immigrants who are being terrorized by these gangs.

Casey:

> They're coming into low-income cities, and they're going to take your children. They're going to indoctrinate them with the gang culture, and then we're going to see the gang war that we had back in the 1980s revisit us again here. I mean, the border needs to be protected by all means.

Laura Ingraham:

> What you saw and what you lived day in and day out is still happening in Chicago, Manassas, Virginia. Horrific murders. Prince William County. Long Island. These gang rivalries are popping up all over the country now. The more porous the border is, the more opportunity for people to sneak in. What do you think about what Latinos believe about safe streets and a better economy?

Casey Diaz:

> Here's something I'll throw at you. Many of the guys that I ran in the streets with and were in prison with, who came out and successfully completed parole and got a job and started a business out here and started to pay taxes, they're all conservatives now, and the media and the left will not tell you that.

Laura Ingraham:

> Casey, your book is fascinating. It's up on my Facebook page and on lauraingraham.com. Thank you for being here tonight and telling your story.

Casey:

> Thank you so much.

Three minutes and twenty-three seconds flashed by like a lightning strike. When we went to a commercial break, Laura stood up as I got out of my chair and gave me a warm hug. I thanked her for the great day.

It was getting close to 11 p.m., and I was bushed. Joel drove us straight back to the hotel. We all needed sleep since the following day promised to be just as helter-skelter.

Before dawn, right around 5 a.m., I received a knock on my door, stirring me from a deep sleep.

"Casey, it's me," said Mical in a muffled voice.

As if in a trance, I threw some pants on and stumbled to the door.

"What are you doing?" I asked, still out of it.

"Meet me in Joel's room. Hurry."

"Then let me take a shower."

"No, no, no. Just brush your teeth or whatever you have to do, and then meet me at Joel's room."

We had rooms on the same floor, which made things simpler.

I groggily complied. When I walked over to Joel's room, his door was open. He was sitting in front of a room desk with two laptop computers before him. Mical stood next to him. Ear-to-ear smiles creased their faces.

"What's up, man?" I asked. "What's the rush all about."

Joel tilted one of the screens in my direction. "Take a look. *The Shot Caller* is No. 1 on Amazon."

"Is that a good thing?"

"It's not a good thing; it's a great thing. Dude, you knocked Michelle Obama out of first place!"

"Oh, I guess that's a good thing."

"Everyone at Harper's is going bananas. We think it all has to do with last night's interview with Laura."[6]

---

6 Joel was referring to Michelle Obama's autobiography, *Becoming*. Since the Amazon rankings are based on sales in real time and change several times a day, my moment at No. 1 on Amazon would be short-lived—just a few hours. But what a ride.

Mical came alongside me, beaming as we regarded each other. Something special was happening here.

Something only God could orchestrate through remarkable and obedient people like Mical Pyeatt.

WHAT ABOUT THAT DINNER?

I believe Laura Ingraham meant it when she said she'd love to meet my family over a meal in Los Angeles. I'm not sure why she wanted to break bread with me, but I later learned she is a single mom to three internationally adopted children. Her oldest, Maria, was adopted from Guatemala, and two sons, Michael and Nikolai, came from Russia. The older two are in high school, and the youngest, Nikolai, is in middle school.

Did she want to speak to me about life in Central America since I was born in El Salvador? Learn more about the inner workings of a gang? Have an impact on her kids as a father figure since she's a single-parent mom who never married?

I don't know the answers, but I know that a year after our interview, Covid-19 turned this country upside down and changed everything, so she has total grace from me. I imagine Laura is sticking close to her home in McLean, Virginia, and hasn't needed to come to LA.

But Laura, if you do come to Southern California, I hope your invitation is still on the table. You'd love to meet Sana and our three children.

chapter two

A BROTHERLY BOND

by Mical Pyeatt

You've seen my name mentioned several times, and I imagine you're wondering: *Who is this guy?*

Next, you're probably curious about how to pronounce my name. Answer: *Michael Pyeatt like Hyatt.* My surname is Olde French in origin and roughly means "Little bird."

Now that's dispensed with, let's get to my story of how I came alongside Casey to help him share his *Shot Caller* story, which I knew in my heart could impact millions if God opened the right doors. It's been quite a ride for both of us.

Casey and I met because our daughters—Lea for me and Samantha for Casey—were classmates and best buds at the Village Christian School in nearby Sun Valley. They started in kindergarten together, and throughout the early elementary years, Lea and Samantha were inseparable, hanging out after school and doing sleepovers at each other's homes. I was always struck by the incredible sparkle and light on Samantha's face. You could see the little spirit in there.

Casey? I would meet him in passing at school functions. We were cordial to each other, but that was about it. My wife, Sandra, was good friends with Sana, Casey's wife, but the four of us didn't socialize. I was busy with my part of life, which was running a financial services company, and Casey had his sign shop.

We didn't have much in common except for raising children the same age. I was also nineteen years older than Casey and born in Los Angeles in the 1950s, a time when LA was predominantly white. My fair skin turned beet red whenever I surfed Staircase Beach in Malibu, while Casey, a native of El Salvador, was a typical Latino from Central America—shorter in stature and brown-skinned. But we got along in the melting pot that was Los Angeles and shared a sarcastic sense of humor and the same Christian values.

Late one summer afternoon—this would have been sometime in 2012—I happened to drive past Casey's sign shop after visiting my mother, who lived a block-and-a-half away in a leafy neighborhood. Mom was moving into the last parts of her life and was having physical problems, so I'd check in on her a couple of times a week.

I passed Casey's shop on Magnolia Boulevard—the main drag in Burbank—and noticed an Open sign but kept right on driving. Then a thought came to me: *I could give him some business.*

I needed some signage for several interior walls inside my place of business—Primerica, which specializes in providing insurance, investment, and financial services to middle-income families. I had probably four hundred independent agents who worked with me. Eighty percent were part-time since they were commissioned-based, but the go-getters, those making financial services a career and working full time, occupied cubicles inside my Burbank office. I had thirty or forty of those folks. I had recently selected a sales theme for the coming year—"Everyone Deserves a Second Chance." Hence the need for signage.

I drove around the block and dropped in on Casey to see if he could help me. We talked about what I wanted, and he listened well, taking notes. Sure enough, he was the right guy, and his prices were reasonable. We got it all figured out.

The conversation drifted off, a signal that we were done. When I stood up, Casey had a funny look on his face.

"I need to tell you my story," he said.

That was odd to hear, especially in a business setting. Curiosity got the best of me, however. I plopped back down in my chair. "Fine. Tell me your story," I said.

For the next hour, I was transfixed while listening to the basic contours of the *Shot Caller* story. How he arrived in Los Angeles as a toddler, the oldest son of immigrants from El Salvador fleeing a civil war. Witnessing a double homicide as an eight-year-old boy when three gang members were assassinated in a dark alley behind his family's apartment. Joining a gang at eleven and being directed to stab a wounded gang member with a flat-edged screwdriver. The home invasions. Ransacked apartments. Binding terrified victims with ropes and covering their mouths with duct tape. Cruising the neighborhood, looking for rival gang members roaming on turf belonging to his homies, the Rockwood Street Locos.

"I liked capturing them and sticking it to them," Casey said about adversarial gang members.

I'd never met a former gangbanger before, so I was mesmerized as he related one disturbing story after another about being a "shot caller"—the power broker who determined who got hurt or killed inside and outside prison walls. I couldn't imagine what it was like being tossed into a solitary confinement cell at New Folsom State Prison, where human contact was severely restricted and the guards remained mute unless it was absolutely necessary to speak with him.

But then his remarkable, gritty story took an unexpected turn when he talked about seeing a movie about his life on the wall inside his prison cell. That was a supernatural event on steroids.

When Casey came to the part about Jesus looking at him and saying, "Darwin, I'm doing this for *you*," I interrupted him.

"Who's Darwin?" I asked.

"That's my legal name. Casey is a nickname. But that was the moment I realized Jesus Christ was nailed to that cross for all my sins and for hurting so many people. I fell to my knees on the rock-hard concrete floor and asked God to forgive me."

There was more to the story, of course. When Casey finished, I walked out of his sign shop, asking myself, *What did I just hear?*

That happened on a Wednesday. I thought about what he said that evening and into Thursday. Friday, too. I couldn't get him out of my mind all weekend. Then on Monday morning, Casey arrived at my office to install a half-dozen signs throughout the building.

Casey didn't know that I had a longstanding "manager's meeting" at nine a.m. in the conference room that was part business and part team building every Monday morning. Sometimes, I'd share an inspirational story to raise everyone's spirits.

Wait a minute. What story could be more uplifting than what Casey had told me?

I found him wearing beige work clothes perched on a ladder in the main hallway. "Casey, I got a quick question," I began. "We're having a Monday morning meeting in a few minutes. Could you tell my colleagues the same story you told me the other day?"

Casey didn't hesitate. "Sure, of course."

Right at 9 o'clock, probably two dozen of my agents filed into the conference room. They were a diverse group of people, reflecting LA's population mix. Some were churchgoers interested in spiritual matters, but probably half weren't.

After going through a few agenda items, I introduced Casey in this manner: "Because we're in the business of 'second chances' and helping people change, I would like you to listen to a story I heard last week that was the most powerful presentation that I've heard in a long time. His name is Casey Diaz, and he owns a local sign shop. You may have seen him hanging up some new signs this morning. Casey, the floor is yours."

Casey rose from the chair next to mine and took his place at the head of a long table. I slipped to the rear to be a fly on the wall and observe how people responded. My wife, Sandra, was there that day. She sat opposite me. I always encouraged her to be there for the Monday morning manager's meeting so she could see what we were doing.

As Casey began relating his gripping story, a thought came to mind: *Why isn't this a book or a movie?* His tale certainly had all the earmarks of a Hollywood blockbuster. Meanwhile, I kept tabs on how people were reacting. Like me a week earlier, I could tell they were thoroughly engaged and listening closely.

Then something happened twenty to twenty-five minutes into his presentation that would change my life. It happened when I heard God's voice speak to me clearly and distinctly: *I want you to help this man get his story out.*

I hadn't had God speak to me like that since He called my name during an altar call at a church camp when I was twelve.

✦ ✦ ✦

I grew up in the Crenshaw district of Los Angeles, where my father, Thomas Pyeatt, was pastor of the First Church of God. I was the oldest of three boys and under the spotlight as a pastor's kid—a PK. We lived in a parsonage on the church property, so we were always visible.

Crenshaw's neighborhoods were mixed-race in my early years, white and black, but the population changed to primarily black in the early 1960s as white families moved to the San Fernando Valley. The black community in Crenshaw at the time was very family-centered,[1] so it shocked me when I sat on a curb next to a little black friend of mine. He looked despondent.

"My dad is leaving," he said.

"Where's he going?"

"I don't know. I don't think he's ever coming back."

This was shocking news because I'd never heard of a family experiencing divorce.

Then our family was rocked, not by Dad and Mom splitting up, but by my father learning he had brain cancer. Doctors gave him twelve months to live, but he submitted to a series of operations on the brain that kept him alive for eight more years. Most of my memories are not of him at the church, where he was a faithful pastor and teacher, but of watching him go in and out of hospitals. When he died, I was in the ninth grade.

Mom, a stay-at-home mom her entire marriage, was a real-life June Cleaver who wore calf-length dresses and white pearls. Suddenly, we had to leave the parsonage, so she moved us to Burbank because she had friends there who could offer emotional support. Fortunately, my father had term life insurance, which provided enough money for Mom to buy us a house in Burbank and go to night school to become a nurse. She would graduate at age forty-two with a nursing degree.[2]

We moved into our new place two days before I started my 10th-grade year at Burrows High. I was shocked at how I was surrounded by so many white kids compared to Crenshaw. At my new high school, there was only one black girl—an exchange student from Africa.

I was a troubled kid during my high school years and very angry

---

1 Unfortunately, this would change in the mid-1960s with the passage of the "Great Society" legislation creating new welfare programs that penalized married couples with children, leading to a substantial rise in homes without fathers.

2 Upon earning her degree, Mom went to work at Children's Hospital, where she worked for twenty years and retired financially independent, doing it all by saving and investing.

at God for taking my father. Deep pain followed me everywhere. I stopped going to church, and my mom didn't have the heart or the energy to fight me. Even though I had accepted Jesus as my Lord and Savior at a summer camp when I was twelve, all my faith fell away.

Besides, I only wanted to work on weekends to make some money. On Saturday morning, I'd walk over to a car wash on Magnolia Boulevard, where they paid me $25 a day in cash to dry off cars, which I thought was pretty good. Next, I got my first real job at Dinah's Fried Chicken, a diner on Victory Boulevard in Burbank. I started as a busboy and dishwasher and worked my way up to waiting on tables, where I earned tips. Sometimes, I donned a white apron, cut up twenty-four cases of whole fryers, and then breaded and fried chicken for the customers. I worked all day Saturday and Sunday and built up my bank account.[3]

After graduating high school, I wanted to buy a Triumph Bonneville 650 motorcycle with all the money I made. "Not while you're under my roof," Mom declared.

Screw it. I moved out and into a dump of a place with a friend. I was seventeen years old and entirely on my own.

Everyone said I needed to attend college, so I enrolled at the local community college, Valley JC. I didn't like the first day. On the second day, at lunchtime, I quit. What was my plan? Work at a body shop.

I learned how to spray-paint cars and pound out fenders and then got a job at A.E. Johnson's Corvette shop in North Hollywood. I'd been working on shiny 'Vettes for a year when a friend asked me if I wanted to work at Universal Studios in the garage, servicing the trams that ferried the tourists on tours of the back lots. Then I began driving trucks to movie shoots, which meant a lot of sitting around. I was in the film business, remember?

---

3 I also started working two or three days a week after school, so I was probably clocking in twenty, twenty-five hours a week during my last two years of high school. That's all I wanted to really do—work and earn money.

With time to kill, I made sure I had a book or two in the cab. I liked reading biographies and autobiographies of successful people, but after flipping through a dozen or two of those, it occurred to me they all told the same story: *I tried something. I failed. I got back up. I tried again, and even though there were more setbacks, I won.*

Feeling like I needed a greater purpose in life, I started going to church again. A young preacher named John MacArthur had started Grace Community Church in Sun Valley. I thought he was one heck of an expositor. Listening to John MacArthur made me feel like I was on the right path.

✦ ✦ ✦

In the wintertime of 1982, I found myself on the back lot at Universal Studios, on a New York street known as "Sting Alley," where the hit movie *The Sting* starring Paul Newman and Robert Redford was filmed. We were on winter hiatus, so nobody was shooting on the lot.

I pulled my pickup truck up to a sidewalk, parked, and stepped outside. I saw a staircase leading to a "New York" brownstone and sat on the steps. I took stock of where I was in life. I was twenty-nine years old, having worked the last nine years at Universal and going nowhere fast. I sat there and wiped back tears. "Please, God. Get me outta here. I hate this. Really hate it. The values are no good. I can't do this the rest of my life."

And then I made a bargain with God. "Lord, I want to work around people with the same values as me. I would like to do something good for people, but first, I need to find out what kind of talents You've given me that I haven't worked on developing. And one more thing: I'd happily work for half the money I'm making now."

Four or five months later, a guy called me about looking at a business he was involved in. *Yeah, yeah, sure I will,* I blathered. We'd make an appointment to meet, and then I'd blow him off.

This happened thirteen times until I finally met with him three months later. He wanted me to join A.L. Williams, a company that sold term life insurance and advised its clients to "invest the rest."[4]

I had much to learn about the financial services world, but I was game. Though it took six months to extricate myself from Hollywood, I eventually opened my own office and became exceedingly successful with A.L. Williams. Fourteen years passed, and I married a wonderful woman named Sandra. We had a honeymoon baby and popped out kids every two years. We purchased a beautiful four-bedroom home on a foothill overlooking Burbank and attended Hollywood Presbyterian Church, where I was a Sunday school teacher.

Life was such a joy ride.

✦   ✦   ✦

I was talking to the Lord while Casey continued telling his story to my work colleagues.

How can I help Casey when I don't know if his story is true? I don't know him that well, I complained.

And then I heard His voice again, this time even clearer and more distinct: *I want you to help this man get his story out.*

I didn't have time to help Casey. I had five kids, a challenging business, a wife, and various responsibilities. *I can't run off on some adventure project,* I told the Lord.

His reply: *I want you to help this man get his story out.*

But Lord, I don't have any ability to do that! I'm just a financial services guy.

I looked across the table at Sandy. Her eyes were glued on Casey as he reached an emotional time in the story—when he saw the movie of his life on a prison wall and asked a guard if he could see a chaplain. Casey said the request stunned the correctional officer. The Shot Caller was asking to see a padre?

---

4 A.L. Williams, founded by Art Williams, would later be sold to New York-based Primerica.

Tears were streaming down both sides of Sandra's face. Watching her, I felt grateful for our marriage and the family God had given me.

And then the Lord's voice was in my head again: *I want you to help this man get his story out.*

This was the *fourth* time I heard God repeat this sentence. On this occasion, though, it felt more like a command than a request. As I considered how to respond, I understood that helping Casey get his story out would mean investing time and money. Regarding the latter, I knew I was in a better financial position than he was.

I bowed my head and searched my heart. God was asking me to do something *way* out of my comfort zone. So why was I resisting?

I wasn't sure, but if He asked me directly *four* times, then I should step out in faith. I looked around to ensure no one was looking and bowed my head. In my heart, I said three simple words to the Lord: *Ok, I will.*

When Casey's talk was over, I met with him and Sandra in my office. I could see that my wife was still emotional and raw. She told Casey, "I feel like I have one foot in and one foot out. Would you pray for me?"

"Certainly," Casey replied, and he prayed over her right there. I thought I was witnessing an incredible moment that drew me closer to Sandra.

As Casey left and Sandy departed, we all went on with the rest of our day. When I arrived home that evening, however, her attitude had flipped 180 degrees. Instead of talking about what an amazing testimony she had heard, she was saying things like, "You don't even know if this guy's for real. What if he's making up his story?"

When I mentioned that she'd been friends with Sana and Casey for quite a while, which had to count for something, she waved that off. "I don't know what to think," she said, "but you need to find out more about him."

I wasn't in a wait-and-see mode. I *knew* I had heard from God directly, and He wouldn't ask me to help someone with a bogus story. But I didn't tell Sandy that, not after that negative reaction.

✦   ✦   ✦

It didn't take long for our lives to spiral out of control.

A couple of weeks after Casey spoke at my office, my oldest daughter, Chelsie, came home from college with her boyfriend in tow and told me she was pregnant. What I haven't mentioned is that Chelsie was my first child from a previous marriage. When Sandy and I tied the knot, Chelsie was five years old. To her credit, Sandra had been a loving stepmom and had a special mother-daughter relationship with Chelsie.

As I digested this unexpected news, I knew I wanted to support my daughter, especially after Chelsie said she had no intention of aborting the child. I thought this unplanned pregnancy might bring our family closer together, which can happen in situations like this. But first, Sandra needed to hear this news directly from Chelsie.

The following day, I invited Sandra and Chelsie to come to my office. After everyone took a seat, Chelsie broke the news about her pregnancy to her stepmother, who listened intensely. Sandra handled the situation with poise. After thinking a bit, she offered to host a shower for Chelsie, so I was pleased to see the positive reaction from my wife. When they both walked out together, I sat at my desk and thought, *Okay, good. This will work out.*

Later that day, Sandra called and said we needed to go out to dinner and talk. We could do spur-of-the-moment things like that because Sandy's mother, a widow named Nancy, lived with us. Nancy would make dinner and help the kids finish their homework until we came home.

But the tone in Sandra's voice unsettled me. I almost didn't recognize her on the phone because it was so off. Rattled, I kept the conversation short, called our office chaplain, David Grant, and asked him to pray for me.[5] I felt very uncomfortable in my spirit about what I had heard.

I felt even more ill at ease when I saw Sandra march into the restaurant and slip into the booth we were sharing. Sandy's a petite woman, just five feet, two inches, but when she sat down, I saw a big, mean, powerful person who was there to read me the riot act regarding my oldest child.

And Sandra did, angrily telling me that we had to separate Chelsie from our four children because she was pregnant out of wedlock. "I don't want Chelsie to have anything to do with our kids," she said. "She's a bad influence, and I don't want her around."

I was in shock. Sandy and I had been together for seventeen years, but I felt like I didn't know her anymore.

No sooner had we gotten home when her mother also lit into me. That didn't surprise me because my mother-in-law was a busy-body, way too much in our business. As the harangues continued without letup over the next month or so, I reached the point where I pressured Nancy to move out and sweetened the deal by renting her an expensive apartment in Burbank.

Suddenly, I was coming home from work to an empty house because Sandra and our four children lived most of the time at my mother-in-law's place. Sandra would bring the kids back and forth to our house so I could see them, but kids talk. I found out that a guy Sandra's age was showing up at dinner time and hanging out there. Then he was spending the night. It didn't take much to figure out that my wife was getting involved with a guy who was *living* at my mother-in-law's apartment . . . that I was paying for!

My family life disintegrated overnight. Neither Sandy nor her mother would admit that she was having an affair over the next eighteen

---

5 I employed an office chaplain because we were in a business that dealt with a lot of people, and some of those people needed personal counseling—stuff that was way above my pay grade.

months. I had a prayer team of five people, including Casey and David Grant.[6] They were praying for me, but I believed I was losing a battle that felt very much like spiritual warfare. Everything was a mess—my emotions, my spiritual life, my business, which was having its own set of problems, and my health. I was passing out because of low blood pressure and was lucky to be alive, a doctor told me. I ended up in the hospital with cardiomyopathy, also called the "broken heart syndrome," and left the hospital with a newly installed pacemaker.

Whenever I had the kids over, I felt a demonic presence inside the house, like a satanic being was looming over my children as they sprawled together on the couch, watching TV. It was spooky.

Then Sandra got a court order to get me out of the house. There was nothing I could do to fight it. I had to move out, and my wife and children, my mother-in-law, and my wife's boyfriend moved back in. Locks were changed.[7]

Amid this madness, I was trying to help Casey get his story out there. I'd call various churches and talk to the pastor in charge of the men's ministry, telling him I had a terrific speaker for their next meeting. I got him several bookings, which turned out to be impactful. In addition, Casey was a real buddy during my time of crisis: I don't know what I would have done without him being there for me.

At the same time, it didn't take either of us long to figure out my life started falling apart the moment I said, "Ok, I will" to the Lord. Clearly, the enemy did not want Casey's story to get out there.

Next, I hired Michael Petrone, an experienced actor and screen-writer, to write a screenplay about Casey's story. I also paid him to direct and produce a ten-minute trailer made with a cast and crew,

---

6 The others that I am indebted to are David Glidden, Ruth Chavez, and Marco Renoso.

7 What a brutal, ugly process our divorce would become. Sandra would go through four sets of attorneys in four years and burn through hundreds of thousands of dollars in legal fees to prove . . . what? The worst part was losing "dad time" every day with my children, which hurt all of us and still does.

but after everything was put together in a nice promotional package, we couldn't get any traction. On the book side, I couldn't find a writer despite beating the bushes. It was like no one wanted to touch Casey.

Still, we persevered. At least we had a trailer and a script—something to show anyone in the entertainment industry who would listen. All we needed was that one big break.

Then an entertainment agent called. Said he had heard about Casey's story and wanted us to come to his office. We had a friendly chat, and he seemed very interested, even excited after hearing the short version of Casey's story. He talked a pretty good game about what he could do for us—saying he could get us in front of the right producers and the right filmmakers to get things off the ground.

This led to several more meetings with the agent. He even wined and dined us at his home, where we met his charming family. A friendship was building. I had heard that relationships were how things happened in Hollywood. And now we had one.

Eventually, he asked to see a copy of the script. Said he wanted to go over it and see what shape it was in.

A few days later, Casey and I were invited to his gleaming office in Pasadena, where a lot of deal-making agents live.

"This could be it," I tell Casey, who was taking it all in.

A receptionist led us to the conference room, lined with mahogany wood. A door opened, and the agent walked in and dropped the screenplay on the long rectangular table.

"Nope, we're not doing it," he announced. "We don't like anything about this, so get out. Now. Right this minute."

Casey and I looked at each other. Was this some sort of cruel joke, especially after all the initial interest? And now we were being thrown out of the building.

We stood up to go, but at the door, I reached into my pocket and pulled out my parking ticket. "Hey, do you guys validate?"

"Get out!"

By the time we arrived at the hallway elevator, Casey and I were laughing our heads off.

"I guess we're not doing anything with those people," I joked, my dark humor side coming out.

"It wouldn't appear so," Casey chuckled.

✦　✦　✦

My sales training would not let me give up. Besides, I was used to rejection.

One afternoon, I was having my hair cut by Armand Laliberte, who'd been trimming my hair for more than forty years. Armand graduated from our rival school, Burbank High, at the same time I did, so we knew many of the same people.

As he snipped away, he asked me what I was up to, and I mentioned how I was trying to help Casey get his story out there, which led me to telling a short version of the *Shot Caller* story.

A few days later, a fellow named Bob Hastings was in Armand's chair. Bob and I both attended Burrows High at the same time (I was a grade or two older). Bob was a lifelong client of Armand, just like me.

"Mical Pyeatt was in here," Armand said as he worked his scissors.

"Oh, what's he up to?" Bob asked.

Armand related the highlights of Casey's story.

A few weeks later, I was back in Armand's chair, and he told me that he had seen Bob Hastings and had mentioned Casey. Now I had a lead because I'd heard that Bob was the sales director at KKLA, the most-listened Christian radio station in the country.[8]

KKLA, at 99.5 FM on the dial, sold half-hour time slots to various parachurch organizations like Focus on the Family, Insight for Living, and Truth for Life, as well as preachers like my old pastor,

---

8 I knew Bob was at KKLA because I was still friends with Michael Hastings, his older brother and a classmate of mine at Burrows High. Michael was on the Burbank City Council for many years and was the mayor at one time.

John MacArthur. But from Monday through Friday at 4 p.m., KKLA broadcasts a three-hour live talk show program hosted by Frank Sontag known as, you guessed it, the "Frank Sontag Show."

Sontag liked to bring in guests for long-form interviews that either lasted for a fifteen-minute segment or two or the entire broadcast hour. I thought Casey would be a great guest, but I was biased.

I called Bob and asked if I could see him over lunch, knowing I'd have a better chance of getting Casey on the "Frank Sontag Show" if we met in person. During our meal, I shared Casey's story and gave Bob a copy of the screenplay.

When I followed up, Bob told me he hated the screenplay—just like the Pasadena entertainment agent—but he was impressed to hear that Casey was a part-time pastor and how he had turned his life around. Bob not only said he'd put in a good word for me with Frank Sontag, but he also gave me Frank's phone number.

I had to leave an umpteen number of messages on Sontag's phone, but he finally called me back one day. I conferenced in Casey and listened to them go back and forth for a bit. I paid close attention—and prayed—while Frank asked several questions about Casey's gang background and prison time.

I'd listened to Frank many times over the years while driving around LA. He struck me as someone who had been around the block a few times and wouldn't be easily impressed, but after speaking with Casey, I heard Frank utter words that tickled my ears: "Could you come on the show next week?"

This was huge, Frank bringing in Casey for an in-studio interview live on the air. Tens of thousands of Angelenos would be listening during their afternoon commute.

A lot of people are finally gonna hear Casey. Maybe a famous Hollywood producer or someone in the book business on their way home from work will hear the potential in Casey's story during their evening commute.

I was invited to join Casey inside the broadcasting booth, although I was a spectator, not a participant. My ten-year-old son, Tommy, sat beside me, which was also a thrill. As Casey started telling his story, I was fixated on him. I wasn't watching Sontag, who was letting Casey roll with it, with no commercial interruptions. Then Casey came to a very emotional part of his story—and choked up. He couldn't continue.

I turned to Sontag, thinking he would chime in since everyone knows that "dead air" is the terror of radio show hosts and broadcast producers worldwide, but tears were rolling down Sontag's cheeks. He, too, couldn't speak. When I glanced over at the engineer behind the thick window, he was also broken up and a mess.

Four or five long seconds had passed. I started mentally counting *six, seven, eight, nine* . . . I'd say ten or eleven seconds passed before Sontag cleared his throat and apologized for the long break, but what an awesome moment of live radio.

Casey took the whole broadcast hour.[9] When Sontag closed out the show, he was done for the day, so we hung out with Frank and shot the breeze. I saw a green-colored hardback book behind Frank with his picture on the cover. *Light the Way Home* was the title, and Frank was the author.

"You wrote a book," I said, stating the obvious. "We've been trying to do the same with Casey."

Sontag pulled the volume down from the shelf. "Yeah, it came out a year or so ago. I worked with a writer, a guy from San Diego named Mike Yorkey. I thought he did a good job."

---

9 It's interesting to me that we did the "Frank Sontag Show" on Casey's birthday, November 13.

chapter three

HE'S A HERO—FOR ALL OF US
by Mike Yorkey

first heard about Casey Diaz from Mical Pyeatt, who reached out to me by phone. He said Casey had been on the "Frank Sontag Show" and had been given my number from Frank.

After bringing me up to speed on who Casey was—a former gangbanger with an incredible come-to-Jesus story—Mical asked me, "Would you be interested in writing Casey's book?"

Two things about phone calls like this:

1. I depend on the Lord to bring me projects, so I know I'm supposed to listen when I get an unexpected phone call like this. This could be a "divine appointment," as I call it.

2. I receive a dozen or two exploratory phone calls or emails like this every year—people wanting me to write a book for them—but I can't help everybody for a variety of

reasons: the project doesn't fit in my schedule; I don't think they have a book in them, meaning their story or what they have to say is not ready for prime time; or they don't have the money to pay me upfront to write their book.

I usually have two or three books going simultaneously because collaborators like myself (also known as ghostwriters) are freelancers, meaning if we're not writing and editing, we're not eating. So, like general contractors who take on several home remodeling jobs at the same time, we try to juggle several projects simultaneously.

Mical's pitch was enthusiastic, telling me this was the most incredible story ever told and I wouldn't believe it when I heard it. I politely listened because I didn't know if what he was saying was hype or the truth, but I had to admit that I was intrigued by the basic outline: a Los Angeles gangbanger comes to Christ in prison and transforms into a part-time pastor and model citizen. When Mical offered to send me some YouTube videos that Casey had taped and their long-form trailer for a movie they wanted to make, I said, "Sure, I'll take a look."

I'll be honest: I almost walked away from the project after watching the trailer. There was a lot of gory violence—Casey's dad hitting his defenseless wife in the face, fist fights in the 'hood, gang members getting stabbed, and blood streaming down strawberry-bruised faces. It was awful to watch.

The YouTube videos of Casey talking into the camera and telling his story were much better, but I still wasn't getting the entire picture. But I didn't want to tell Mical that I wasn't interested. I asked him if I could think about it, stalling for time.

One thing I liked about the videos from Casey, besides how he struck me as a humble dude who'd been through a lot, was that he spoke mother-tongue English, which is another way of saying that

English was his first language.[1] That would make my job much easier because first-person memoirs are written from interviews with the author. For this book to work, Casey had to not only fully describe what was happening around him, but I needed him to tap into his feelings at that moment in time. This isn't an easy task for anyone, but I felt Casey could do it after we spoke on the phone several times.

What also engaged me about Casey was his deadpan delivery and colorful way of talking, using street slang from a world I didn't know. I grew up in La Jolla, California, a beach town one hundred miles south of downtown Los Angeles as the crow flies. My innocent days of youth were spent riding surf mats and playing tennis at the La Jolla Rec Center. The closest thing we had to a gang were the gnarly surfers who banded together to harass non-locals—"kooks," they called them—out of the lineup.

The fact that Casey was Hispanic and I was white made me want to write the book even more. I had ghosted several books for black artists and athletes, including Marilyn McCoo and Billy Davis Jr.'s autobiography, *Up, Up and Away*.[2] I loved coming alongside these special people and telling their stories. As for Casey, we came from different ethnic backgrounds, but I welcomed the chance to capture his "voice," a term we use in the collaboration world.

The more I thought about it, the more I believed the Latino community needed a Christian hero. I recognized that the demographics, especially in Southern California, had markedly changed during my lifetime, and I was okay with that. But I couldn't think of any Hispanics or Latinos looked up to in the Christian world or placed on a pedestal.

---

1 When I asked Casey if he spoke Spanish, he said he did, but his Spanish "sucked." Hearing him say that endeared him to me even more. While Casey humorously downplays his ability to speak *en español*, he's done a lot of Spanish-language interviews on Univision or Estrella TV and represented himself and *The Shot Caller* book well to the Spanish-speaking community.

2 Marilyn and Billy were part of The Fifth Dimension, a pop group from the late '60s and early '70s best known for their big hit, "Aquarius/Let the Sunshine In." I've also written an unauthorized biography on NBA star Steph Curry that spend a lot of time describing how he grew up.

Sure, there were entertainment celebrities like Jennifer Lopez and Gloria Estefan and baseball stars like Alex Rodriguez and David "Big Papi" Ortiz, but the last Hispanic with an elevated status in the Christian world that I could recall was evangelist Nicky Cruz, also a former gang member. Cruz was the subject of a mega-selling biography, *The Cross and the Switchblade*, with 15 million copies in print, but that book was released in 1963. Cruz was in his late seventies, so I wondered if God had something special planned for Casey—a passing of the torch, if you will.

If He did, I certainly wanted to do my part to help Casey get his story out there.

✦   ✦   ✦

A few months slipped by. I listened to Casey's recordings that he made while sitting on a park bench, talking in a stream-of-conscious manner. While they were interesting, I knew this project wouldn't get going in earnest until we met in person and established a rapport with each other. The only way I could get a sense of who Casey was would be sitting across from one another, looking each other in the eye, and bantering back and forth.

I agreed to meet Casey and Mical halfway between Burbank and my hometown of Encinitas. We chose Costa Mesa in Orange County since my son and his family lived there. While my wife, Nicole, babysat a pair of grandsons, I met Casey and Mical at a Panera restaurant next to South Coast Plaza, a world-famous shopping mall.

As expected, I immediately liked the two guys, who seemed to play off each other and enjoyed joking around. From a book standpoint, I could quickly tell that Casey was a collaborator's dream: he was an excellent storyteller, could recall minute details,[3] and poked fun at

---

3 One time Casey told me he was so bored in solitary confinement that he'd sit on his bed and count holes in the ceiling. "How many holes were there?" I asked. Casey's reply: "I counted 3,680. I can never forget that number."

HE'S A HERO—FOR ALL OF US

himself. As we got deeper into his narrative, which I was taping, I realized that his story was *way* more significant than a simple jailhouse conversion. Pyeatt hadn't been blowing smoke.[4]

I was also captivated by how Casey peppered his sentences with street slang, like when he said he was "catching a chain."

"Wait a minute. What's 'catching a chain'?" I asked.

"That's when you get transferred from one prison to the next. The COs dress you in a four-piece suit and then put you on a Gray Goose. It's called 'catching a chain.'"

"Huh?" My head was spinning.

Casey understood he needed to bring me up to speed, so he broke things down. COs were the correctional officers; four-piece suits were a set of chains that went around his waist, which were then locked to handcuffs around his wrists. Then Casey mentioned that the belly chains—also known as Martin chains—were connected to leg irons around his ankles. The entire get-up was called a "four-piece suit" by the prisoners in orange jumpsuits. As for the Gray Goose, that was the convicts' nickname for the prison transport vehicle—a converted Greyhound bus. Except the bus wasn't gray, Casey pointed out. The bus was painted institutional green.

We also talked about the "business side" of the publishing world. I had a longtime literary agent, Greg Johnson, who represented me, and the way things worked, I needed to write a couple of sample chapters and a comprehensive book proposal that my agent could shop to publishing houses.

I usually charge $5,000 to do that since it takes me two to four months to prepare such a package, but I waived the fee for two reasons:

1. I liked Casey and the story very much. I'd been an

---

4 One thing I noticed about Casey and Mical is that they liked to call people by their last names, which humored me. I'm now known as "Yorkey" to them, which I accept as a term of endearment.

author and collaborator for twenty-five years, so I was at a point in my writing career where I could take risks.

2. I also saw how the wind was blowing: Casey was a part-time pastor with a mom-and-pop sign shop business and a family of five to support: his wife, Sana, and their three growing children. His oldest two, Samantha and Miah, would enter college in several years and suck out any spare cash in his savings accounts.

This direction meant I was working on speculation. If a publisher didn't pick up the book, I would be out of luck.[5] I felt comfortable with the risk . . . well, maybe not that comfortable, but Casey told me I was his guy. That was good enough for me, so I stepped out in faith. We worked together on a handshake deal.[6]

Since I was working on spec, I told Casey and Mical that I'd have to write sample chapters and a proposal in my spare time, which they were fine with. I'd say I took eight months to write four sample chapters that amounted to 10,000 words, plus a thirty-page proposal. The pitch gave an overview of the book and described how Casey was uniquely positioned to promote the book because he could reach the broader American audience when being interviewed on radio and TV or using social media since English was his first language. I knew this was important to Christian publishers because they live in an English-speaking world.

Greg Johnson sent the proposal and sample chapters to several dozen publishers, large and small. The response was the sound of crickets. On one level, I understood why: publishers are not in the hero-making business. They are in the publishing business, which meant there had

---

5 We could have always self-published *The Shot Caller*, but we all agreed we wanted a traditional Christian publisher behind the book, which is like a seal of approval to the public.

6 Eventually, we would put things down in writing, but I worked a long time without a contract because I wanted to do this book.

to be a reasonable expectation that they could make a return on their investment in Casey, which would be in the tens of thousands of dollars.

But something else was in play: I knew that the acquisition editors—the people who can green-light a project—were sitting in comfy offices in New York City and Nashville, the two axis points for the publishing world. Could they identify with a gangland story coming out of the mean streets of downtown Los Angeles? I harbored my doubts.

If Casey got in a conference room with a publisher and a half-dozen acquisition editors at their monthly "committee meeting," I knew the outcome would be different: he'd walk out with a book deal in hand. But that's not how the publishing world does things. They're old school, meaning everyone goes through a proposal and sample chapters process; no in-person pitches are allowed.

After all the major players rejected us, plus the smaller houses, I wasn't giving up. Casey and Mical certainly weren't. They had put five years into this project and were eternal optimists. On this, we were brothers.

By now, I had a good handle on Casey's story and felt I had an excellent beginning, a solid middle section, and a satisfying redemptive ending. If we were to land a book deal, I'd have to write the entire book. Ten thousand words weren't cutting it.

Whenever I had spare time, I worked on more chapters, but it was a slow process. I had two or three compelling projects ahead of Casey that I was contracted for, but I couldn't get him or his story out of my mind.

✦ ✦ ✦

As I parked myself in front of my iMac, I wanted to convey several things, starting with how and why Casey "jumped into" a gang at age eleven—there's that lingo, again—and what he did to climb through the ranks to reach "shot caller" status. Once that was established, I wanted to show how dangerous it was for Casey when he became a Christian in prison and had the guts to inform his fellow Latino gang members that he was following Someone Else now. Casey literally signed his death warrant when he met with gang leaders in the prison yard during their exercise hour. I used that engrossing episode as our "grabber" scene to start *The Shot Caller* and hook readers for what was to come.

As I worked through the chapters, a question haunted me: *How much violence do I share?*

The violence couldn't be over-the-top like the movie trailer or a Stephen King novel, but rival gang members didn't meet for tea and crumpets in the afternoon either. I figured that readers were exactly like me: we had heard about gangs and knew they killed each other over turf wars, but we had never really met a gang member up close and personal, either in person or through a book or a movie. Casey could be the conduit—the person who could tell us what it was really like to be in a gang or prison, where each day could be your last.

Writing is a different medium than film, but I felt we had to be somewhat graphic in a few areas to *show* readers that Casey lived in a scary world of tit-for-tat violence instead of *telling* readers that he did some bad things. As one early reader told us, "I'll never look at screwdrivers the same way again."

To his credit, Casey had no qualms or hesitations in giving me details of his crimes, re-creating conversations with ganglords and prison guards, or describing his roiling emotions at the time. As I said, a collaborator's dream. But I was trying to finish a how-to book on entrepreneurship, an update of the 20th anniversary of *Every Man's Battle*, a rewrite of a diet book (*Portion Your Plate*), and a memoir of Ron Archer, a black pastor. I'd say six months passed without me writing one more sentence.

During the summer of 2017, Mical called to check on my progress and asked politely if I could pick up the pace, so I put things into fourth gear and finished writing the book around Halloween.

This time the entire book went out for a new round with publishers. Once again, everyone passed except for Emanate, a new imprint for Thomas Nelson, one of the leading Christian book companies based in Nashville, Tennessee, and a division of HarperCollins. The head guy at Emanate was Joel Kneedler, a veteran of the Christian book world as a publicist, literary agent, and now publisher.

JOEL KNEEDLER

Since we were a new and smaller imprint within Thomas Nelson, we didn't receive as many pitches as the big publishing houses do. My guess is thirty to forty book proposals arrive each month via email. We only deal with literary agents because they "cull the herd," meaning they don't want to waste their time or our time pitching us with book ideas that have no chance of being published by us.

I'd say 95 percent of the pitches come with a book proposal and two or three sample chapters to give us a flavor of what the book is about and what shape it's in. Casey's proposal was different: we received the entire manuscript, which is a rarity in our industry since many authors are wary of spending six months writing a manuscript—or paying a freelancer to write the book for them—that no publisher wants and never gets published. What caught my eye was seeing Mike Yorkey as the collaborator. I knew from his reputation that the manuscript would be well-written.

We're old school in that we print out all the proposals, sample chapters, and the occasional complete manuscripts, which pile up in a corner of my office. For some reason, I came up with every excuse *not* to read Casey's manuscript and kept dragging my feet. Then one day, I spotted the *Shot Caller* proposal and manuscript and decided to read Casey's opening chapter, which was very dramatic. As someone who grew up in California, I was hooked and wanted to read more. When I eventually found time to read the entire manuscript, I knew it was a winner.

But I needed a second opinion, so I asked a young editor named

Forrest to read it through. When he took the manuscript home that night, I expected to hear from him in a few days. Instead, he waltzed into my office the following morning and announced, "We're going to publish this, right?"

"Why do you say that?"

"Because it's awesome. We need to do more books like this. It's gritty and open in a way that caught my mind and my heart. I loved the way Casey was honest about his encounter with Jesus."

At that point, I knew we would take it to our monthly publishing board meeting, where the editorial side meets with the sales and marketing people to make the final decisions on what we publish and what we cut loose. These salespeople deal day in and day out with the heavy hitters: Amazon Books, Barnes & Noble, Books-A-Million, Christianbook.com, etc. We usually consider three or four books at these meetings.

The fact that Casey didn't have a large social following on Instagram and Facebook was a black check against him, but having a wingman like Mical Pyeatt behind him mitigated that concern. When we showed everyone Casey's testimony on Vimeo, the salespeople saw firsthand how powerful the story was. A vote was taken and approved.

We contacted Greg Johnson with the good news and worked up a contract with deal points to publish *The Shot Caller*. Then our graphic design team went to work coming up with a cover while another editor and I did a fine-tooth "line edit" of the book.

We didn't see much to question or rework.

MIKE

Sometimes the final editing process can be a pain since editors are famous for nitpicking things, but I don't think ten words were changed from the original manuscript.

The only bummer is that we had to wait *an entire year* before the book was released on April 2, 2019.[7] But I knew Casey's life would change dramatically when the book hit #1 on Amazon after *The Ingraham Angle* show, even though it was only for a couple of hours. More importantly, I was confident that people's lives would change, especially as I read reviews on Amazon and elsewhere.[8]

One from John R. Desimone especially touched me:

> For too many years, Christian memoirs have been written with the sympathies of the readers more in mind than the experiences of the writer. The gritty details of the mean-streeted lives are usually elided, deleted, glossed over, watered down, or whatever euphemism you want to use to describe the trouble, the abuse, or the crime some authors have dealt with. Admittedly, the dark places we reach before the light of Christ comes into our lives can be traumatic to talk about.
>
> Casey Diaz's memoir, *The Shot Caller*, pulls no such punches. This is a bare-knuckle read. It would be impossible to tell it any other way. Diaz does not mince words describing his violent acts. His description of his anger, rebellion, rejection, and the travails of a broken boy growing up in a broken home will wrench your heart.
>
> I can certainly empathize with what happened next: a young man looking for affirmation finds his acceptance in street thugs who jump him into their

---

7 Casey was blown away when he heard that the official release date was April 2, 2019, because it was twenty-fifth anniversary of the day when he accepted Jesus into his heart after witnessing a movie-like "screening" of his life and Jesus' crucifixion on the concrete wall opposite his prison cell bunk.

8 There are more than seven hundred reviews on Amazon, which pleases us greatly. Eighty-five percent are five-star and effusive in their praise for Casey and his story.

gang. Acceptance comes through being the most violent, the one another's fear, and it's not long before all semblance of the boundaries of human compassion and respect for life vanished from his conscience. His viciousness has a hair-trigger. It can snap at any moment. And it does. This is not a fluffy story.

It's a wonder he survived to reach his sixteenth birthday. The boy that jumped him in, the one Casey looked up to, died in a drive-by. Incarcerated at the age when most boys are just getting the freedom to drive, Casey ends up the big shot behind bars, the Shot Caller, the one others follow in jail, the one who decides who lives and dies. Heavy stuff for a young kid. Saddled with that reputation, he's transferred to a high-security prison in Northern California, where he's immediately placed in solitary confinement.

Alone. In a dark cement cubical, he only sees the light one hour a day—oh, how the mighty have fallen. He won't see it this way until later in life, but that dark cell is the biggest act of grace God or man could grant him. He's restrained. He's boxed in, cut off from every human voice. He is out of sight and all but forgotten by the prison system. He is beyond the reach of anyone who could help him.

But it just so happens that a black church woman, who had ridden a bus all day from South Central LA to minister to convicts, came into Casey's unit. He could hear her voice down the hall. But his cell is at the far end. No one goes down that far except to drop off a food tray. Casey hears her ask, "Who's down there?" He hears the guard tell her to forget that boy, he's beyond help. But she comes to his door anyway and speaks a few chosen words to him.

Look, I'm not going to spoil the rest of the story. If you enjoy stories of grace and redemption, and even if you don't, this is a worthy read. It's one you can pass along to your friends and family. It's a testimony of two people. One is the faithful churchwoman who regularly came to the jail and spoke the words of grace at the right moment to the right person. And the second is Casey who responded, and God lifted him out of that dark hole and gave him a new family.

Casey also started receiving emails from prisoners, cops, correctional officers, and prison chaplains. All were variations of the same theme: *Casey, your book is changing lives inside the prison.*

That's awesome to hear, and I'll always be grateful to come alongside Casey and help him tell his extraordinary story. But before I exit stage right, I want to share one final thought.

When I decided to help Casey tell his incredible story of faith and redemption, I wanted to give the Hispanic community a hero, someone to look up to.

But when we heard from hundreds and then thousands of people who were blown away by Casey's testimony, God showed me that I was wrong.

Casey Diaz is a hero for everyone.

part 2

THE IMPACT INSIDE PRISONS AND BEYOND

chapter four

CHAP RAP

 by Chaplain Karen Konrad

was watching *The Ingraham Angle* one night when the host, Laura Ingraham, teased her next segment before a commercial break.

"My next guest, Casey Diaz, is a former gang member who served time in prison," the Fox host said. "You'll want to hear his interesting take on what's happening on our southern border when we return."

My ears perked up. A former gang member on national TV? As a prison chaplain at Brown County Jail in Green Bay, Wisconsin, I ministered to gangbangers all day long. I knew from experience how lethal they could be—inside and outside prison walls. So what was a former gang member doing on Laura Ingraham's show? I was eager to find out.

When Laura introduced Casey after the commercial break, the show's producers flashed the cover of *The Shot Caller*.

He's also an author? Now I was really intrigued. Throughout the segment, I was transfixed by Casey's confident, no-nonsense demeanor and his level-headed observation that not every migrant was coming to the US to pick our apples.

As a chaplain—and the only one at the Brown County Jail—I was well aware that thousands and thousands of gang members from Mexico and Central America were slipping through our southern border and committing crimes. Even in a northern state like Wisconsin, gangs used violence and intimidation to control their illegal money-making activities, including robbery, drug dealing, prostitution, human trafficking, and fraud. Following their arrests and convictions, I did my best to reach out to gang members locked up inside the Brown County jail and state and federal prisons in eastern Wisconsin.

After Laura thanked Casey for being on her show, I quickly ordered *The Shot Caller* online. When the paperback arrived, I was hooked from the first page and devoured its contents. What a fantastic read! Casey's inspirational testimony demonstrated God's miraculous power, and his conversion experience reminded me that Jesus can save anyone. When I finished *The Shot Caller*, I believed his astonishing story of redemption could change the lives of prisoners on the inside—the people I ministered to daily.

My belief was so deep that I drove to every Barnes & Noble and Christian bookstore in Green Bay and Brown County and purchased every copy of *The Shot Caller* I could find. I also ordered a case of twenty-four books, with half in Spanish.

Books are good ways to reach inmates who have plenty of free time on their hands. Many prisoners say, "Hey, Chap! Got a good book for me?" Now I had something I could readily recommend. I placed thirty copies in the prison library at the Brown County Jail and scattered a handful of paperback copies inside several state and federal prisons in Wisconsin.

I felt that once inmates read Casey's incredible transformation inside prison walls—and how he sought a prison chaplain after God touched him in his cell—they would trust me. I say that because gang members don't want to talk to chaplains. They view any conversations with a clergy member as a sign of weakness. But when a book I recommended hit the sweet spot for them, I used that experience as a bridge to myself and my programs, like meeting with me one-on-one or joining the worship services I put on inside the prison.

Deep inside their souls, these inmates knew being a gang member rarely ended well, but they didn't see a way out. But now they had a role model in someone they *could* emulate if they wanted to change their lives.

✦ ✦ ✦

Why was *The Shot Caller* such a hit with prisoners? Because Casey's story told it like it really was on the streets and behind bars while offering hope to those living in a caged environment where despair and despondency seep from the prison walls. It wasn't long before word-of-mouth swept through the prison's pods like a prairie fire: *Dude, you have to read this Casey Diaz book. It's crazy, man.*

They told me that the black cover hooked them. Certainly the title *The Shot Caller* spoke their language, but using a font popular in the gang culture—Krakens—and the darkness of the Los Angeles skyline pulled prisoners in. As word seeped out, I couldn't keep Casey's book on the shelf.

I also inserted a copy of *The Shot Caller* into "life packets" that I mailed to prisoners who contacted me. I can't tell you the number of *Shot Caller* books I've sent to inmates who'd written me in the past few years asking for the book, but it's a lot. Inmates can't go to a computer and order a copy from Amazon, so my ministry stood in the gap for them.

Here's another reason *The Shot Caller* was so popular on the inside: many of my readers were gang members from the Los Angeles area who'd been sent to the Midwest by their shot-calling bosses to set up shop and deal drugs, among other vices. They had lived in gang strongholds that Casey described in the book, places like South-Central, Pico-Rivera, and Chinatown. Others had done time in the same prisons that incarcerated Casey.

You couldn't fool these hardened inmates who'd rained death on rivals and were well acquainted with the penal system. They instantly knew that *The Shot Caller* was legit from the opening chapter when Casey described walking out to the exercise yard at New Folsom after being transferred from solitary confinement in the SHU—the acronym for Special Housing Units—to the general prison population. Following three years of segregation, Casey was allowed to interact with fellow prisoners in new surroundings.

Which worried him. There was something Casey needed to tell the shot callers from MS-13, 18th Street, and Florencia 13 waiting for him in the exercise yard: he had become a Christian while in the SHU. He was walking away from gang life. "I feel like I need to tell you this on my first day in mainline so that there are no rumors," Casey wrote.

If you recall from the book, Casey knew that once he was transferred to the rest of the prison population, gang leaders would issue a "green light" on Casey, meaning he would be stabbed to death or strangled at the hands of another gang member.

This is why I loved *The Shot Caller* so much. I knew from personal experience what becoming a Christian often meant for prisoners. For former shot callers like Casey, the penalty was death or, in rarer cases, they would be subjected to random beatings, which could occur so frequently that you *wish* you were dead.

But one inmate—I'll call him Jorge—had a beef with Casey's opening chapter. Jorge didn't believe Casey could be "mainlined" after becoming a Christian because the prison authorities *and* Casey would have known he would have been labeled as a "piece of trash" for turning his back on the gangs. "Pieces of trash" got taken out—killed. Jorge was so adamant that Casey couldn't have been mainlined that he started agitating in the pods, telling anyone who'd give him an ear that Casey and his story were full of @#$%.

I tried explaining to Jorge that Casey didn't turn *against* his gang leaders but simply stated that he had become a Christian and couldn't be part of that lifestyle anymore. Despite my clarification, Jorge wouldn't let go of his point of view, which he shared with everyone he could. He stirred up a hornet's nest.

There was also a gang dynamic that muddied the waters here in Wisconsin. Jorge was a "Northerner," meaning he was from a Northern California gang. He was trying to convince Southerners—rival gang members from Southern California—that he had a lock on the truth. One of those Southerners, called Fili, was a leader from one of Ventura County's most prominent and deadliest gangs—the Colonia Chiques. They were known as the "Colonials" on the street and in prison.

Fili argued Casey was telling the truth, that he'd seen prisoners in the SHU who'd become Christians get released to the mainline population. "That's how things go down in SoCal," Fili told Jorge.

But Jorge kept stirring the pot. If there's one thing COs— correctional officers—don't like, it's an undercurrent of mistrust circulating among prisoners. Guys nitpicking each other. Tossing barbs. Acting macho.

Tempers can overheat quickly in a hostile environment where the threat of violence is always bubbling under the surface. All it takes to set off a prisoner is for a careless word or an aggressive glance to be expressed, and fights break out. Something had to be done to get Jorge to leave it alone, but no one could dislodge him from his opinion.

I thought about what I could do. Then God gave me a great idea: ask Casey to clarify things.

But how do I reach the original Shot Caller?

I Googled his name and discovered he had a website at caseydiaz.net. There was a contact page, so I wrote him, explaining the situation as briefly as possible. Then I sent off the email with my contact information.

Within an hour—around eight o'clock at night my time—my cell phone buzzed. I looked down at the number and saw the area code: 818. I knew the prefix was from LA. Who could be calling me from Southern California?

It turned out to be Casey, who immediately struck me as gracious and down to earth. He told me he had received my email and wanted to set the record straight because he did go into mainline, just as he wrote in the book.

CASEY

I remember my conversation with Chaplain Konrad very clearly. When she mentioned that she'd been a chaplain for more than a decade, I knew she was no rookie. Within a few minutes of conversation, I sensed she was a remarkable person of deep faith who genuinely cared about the inmates she ministered to.

Her email had asked a couple of questions. The first dealt with the inmate questioning my story, who mistakenly thought I was put into a Level III yard at New Folsom. As I explained in *The Shot Caller*, each state prison is designed to house inmates with a security level from Level I to Level IV. The higher the level, the more dangerous the inmate.

New Folsom was not a Level III prison; it was a maximum-security Level IV with more staff and armed officers inside and outside the facility. Within Level IV and only Level IVs are the SHUs, where I was put upon my arrival.

"New Folsom doesn't have a III yard, only a IV yard," I told Chaplain Konrad. "By a miraculous reason by which only God knows, I was led out of the SHU after three years, and yes, I was placed in mainline in the IV yard."

The chaplain and I talked that through a bit longer since I wanted her to feel comfortable telling the inmate about our conversation. But there was a second question to be dealt with: Jorge was also saying that I was placed in cells with prisoners from other races, which was totally wrong.

"Nowhere in the book did I say that," I explained. "I was never placed in a cell with another race, either in state prison or the LA County Jail gang module. Shortly after I was sentenced by the court and sent to CYA,[1] they put me in a cell with a white inmate, but that was only for a short time. CYA is different from state prison. Different prison politics."

KAREN

When a book like *The Shot Caller* comes along, its positive message can spread swiftly inside the prison system because everybody needs hope to get through another day in the lockup.

I've seen *The Shot Caller* reach into state and county prisons in Wisconsin and the federal prison system. At the county level, 10,000 inmates pass through our system each year, so Casey's story has impacted thousands since it came out in 2019. I can readily tell when *The Shot Caller* sweeps through a pod: the inmates start talking to each other at the tables in the pod, analyzing and self-reflecting. Plus, the book never makes it back to my personal library.

But it's just not prisoners whose hearts are changed. I've given dozens of copies to COs and administrative staff. When captains, lieutenants, and correctional officers read *The Shot Caller*, they look at prisoners differently: they can view them as people. They better understand why gangs recruit eleven- and twelve-year-olds and how these kids were traumatized by violence at such an impressionable age.

✦　✦　✦

1　CYA stands for California Youth Authority, which is the correctional system for the state's most serious juvenile offenders. I was sixteen at the time.

CASEY

Isn't Chaplain Karen remarkable? We had a follow-up conversation in which she asked me several questions. I thought reading our back-and-forth would be instructive to help you better understand the world I came from and the world she lives in.

Karen

I'm sure you know this, Casey, but one thing I've always seen with gang members is that they can submit to authority in a gang, but the higher-ranking guys seem to struggle with surrendering to Christ because they want to do things their way. That has always struck me as odd, especially with the level of respect they show each other. What will help them understand that they will either bow down now or bow down later?

Casey

Whenever I talk to some of these higher-up guys in the gangs who are in prison, one of the things they respect big-time is when you just give it to them straight up. They're past the cotton candy and the softness of the message. They want you to be direct with them.

When I get a chance, I share heaven, but I mainly talk about the consequences of their sin and the reality of hell waiting for them. "If you think life in this eight-by-ten is bad, you ain't seen bad yet," I'll say.

When they hear straight talk like that, it's almost like the reality of what's waiting for them in eternity hits them in the face. Often, a switch turns on. When I see that happen, I know it's the Holy Spirit working them over. I can see them thinking, *Oh, no. I've got to do something.*

That's when the questions come, which generally fall

along these lines:

- "Can God really save me from all the crimes I've committed?"
- "How can God forgive me for everything I've done?"

Without going into too much detail here, I'll take out my Bible and walk them through several verses on salvation, explaining that we've all sinned and fallen short (Romans 3:23), but God so loved the world that He sent His son to die for our sins and whoever believes in Him shall not perish but have eternal life (John 3:16). But if you declare with your mouth that "Jesus is Lord" and believe in your heart God raised Him from the dead, then you will be saved (Romans 10:9).

I would say that 75 percent of these gang members come to Christ on the spot—the gospel message hits them that hard.

Karen

Can they walk it out then, Casey? Have you *seen* them walk it out?

Casey

Oh, yeah. Plenty of guys become law-abiding and stay law-abiding when they get out. I have guys right now that I'm mentoring who are part of my Bible class. They were Level IV guys, but they're gentle in spirit now. They recognize God gave them a second chance and don't want to blow it.

But I remember this one guy who was part of an organization within the CDC walls with a shot-caller status like me. When he came out, he dropped by my sign shop after hours. All my employees had left the shop, so it was just him and me sitting at a break table. I'll call him Carlos.

"Listen, let's get real," I began. "If you get pulled over, and you've done something illegal out there, the likelihood of you never getting out again will be the consequence of your sin. Because you didn't learn your lesson. That's the reality.

"Dude, you and I have been at the top. People answered to us. We were young cats running amok, and homies listened or faced the consequences. But you just finished fifteen years. You're in your late thirties. You're putting everything at risk to call shots for what—a bunch of sixteen-year-olds? Twenty-year-olds?

"What do you need that for? And if you end up in court in front of a judge and he gives you a life sentence, at some point, some young buck, some young gang member, is going to want your position inside the prison. He will do whatever it takes to take you out. And you know that. For what? There's nothing for you to prove to anybody."

Carlos was listening to me. I could tell he was processing my blunt talk. Then he leaned in and spoke into my ear, like we were still in a prison yard. That's how fresh out he was. I heard him whisper, "This is all legal, right?"

I knew he was referring to my sign shop.

Because we ran together one time, he couldn't see me doing something legal like owning a sign shop. He couldn't put that together. It didn't compute.

"Dude, what you see is the real deal," I said. "Now that I'm a Christian, I'm out of the game and have been since I was at New Folsom. My attitude has been whatever happens, happens. This is who I am, man."

Carlos nodded, thoughtful.

I took a moment to tell him about the 8 a.m. Sunday school class that I teach with my wife, Sana.

"I'd like you to come. But you have to get there early. If you don't arrive by 7:20 or 7:30, you're not getting a seat. You'll end up in the hallway, listening as best as you can."

"What?" A puzzled look came over his face.

"Yeah, about eighty show up every Sunday morning, and we can barely get half of them in the classroom."

The following Sunday, I pulled into the church parking lot shortly after seven o'clock. "Is that your friend?" Sana asked, pointing toward one of the few cars in the lot.

That morning marked a new beginning for Carlos. He started coming to our Bible study every Sunday morning and then staying for the main service, taking in Pastor's preaching and teaching, but I knew he was still a full-on member of the organization, doing dirt.

One Sunday morning, I stood in the sanctuary during worship, singing with my wife and children on my left and Carlos on my right.

I had my eyes closed. The worship team was doing its thing. My hands were raised. I was worshipping the Lord; that's all that matters to me. That's what I was there for.

The next thing I knew, I heard sobbing to the right of me. Just as I turned, Carlos grabbed my shoulder. He was full-on weeping.

"Casey, look at me. What's going on here?" he cried out.

"That's the Holy Spirit convicting you of all your sins. This is your moment. Just surrender to Jesus, man. Give it all up."

That day, Carlos was born again.

A week later, on Saturday morning, he called me. "I'm

meeting some of the guys," he began with a tremor in his voice. "If anything happens to me, you'll know why."

I knew he had two preschool-age daughters, so the weight of the world was on his shoulders.

"You want me to go with you?" I don't know why I said this, but I did.

"No, no, no, bro. You got a family. At one time, you told them you were a Christian and couldn't do this anymore. It's time for me to do this myself. I just wanted to say thank you for sharing Jesus with me, and whatever happens at this meeting, it's all good."

I told Carlos his call touched me, and I prayed for him over the phone.

That was a long Saturday afternoon, waiting for him to call back. I didn't know what was going to happen. Then my phone buzzed.

"Well, what did they tell you?" I asked, eager for a reply.

"Same thing they told you. 'Don't ever come back. Because if you do, we'll take care of you.'"

We both knew what that meant: *We'll kill you.*

Karen

I love what you said about keeping it real. You know, I've had some tough conversations over the years, Casey, because being the only chaplain for 800 prisoners, mostly men, is hard stuff. I've also gotten a lot of heat from pastors that I shouldn't be going in there because I'm a woman. But I don't see anybody else going in very often.

I've wrestled with Jesus about my calling, asking Him for His eyes to love them, to see them the way He sees them. I've had old priests locked up for being pedophiles and gang members wanting to jump them because here in Wisconsin, Casey, they mix all the prisoners: whites, blacks, Latinos, and pedophiles. A lot of bad things can happen.

But your story in *The Shot Caller* has helped so much inside the prisons here, especially when I had former gang members come to the Lord and protect an old priest from getting jumped in the gym. I'm still buying copies, still sharing them with prisoners because they all tell me the same thing: Casey's story is legit.

Casey

I'm humbled. All I can say is, "Thank you, Chap."

✦ ✦ ✦

Chaplains like Karen Konrad are on the front lines of prison ministry. These unsung heroes lead group services, provide guidance and counseling, and console inmates who cannot attend the funeral of a loved one or one of their homies. Their reward will be great in heaven.

Chap has one more story about Fili, the high-level West Coast gangbanger who had my back when Jorge raised a stink. You can read all about it in the next chapter.

chapter five

FILI'S STORY

by Chaplain Karen Konrad

L et me tell you more about Fili, who backed me up when Jorge and I got into it on whether Casey was "mainlined" and allowed to live with other prisoners—and former rivals—after he came out for Christ. Fili must have told Jorge a half-dozen times that Casey's story was on the level.

Fili entered our system at the end of 2015 because of one of the largest drug busts in Green Bay history. He was arrested and charged with eight felonies and five misdemeanors ranging from manufacturing and delivery of amphetamines and marijuana to possession of cocaine and carrying a firearm, something he wasn't allowed to do since he was a convicted felon. At one time, he was among the leadership that had a thousand gang members under them on the West Coast. Whenever the LA cops picked up Fili, they locked him up in the "dungeon" or "the hole"—solitary confinement—just like they did with Casey.

Following his arrest in Green Bay, Fili was heading toward another long stint behind bars. Because of his "priors" and the fact that he was a second-generation leader of a notoriously ruthless Mexican gang in Ventura County north of LA, Fili was looking at a six-to-nine-year sentence. Because so many people were caught up in the bust, it was taking the court system forever to finalize Fili's punishment. The authorities decided to park him at Brown Country Jail. This is where I came into the picture.

When I met him, Fili struck me as a humble and quiet individual, even respectful of authority, but he carried the vibe that you didn't want to mess with him. Despite the bravado, I could tell he was struggling with the idea of being imprisoned for a long time again.

While marking time in Brown County Jail, Fili became interested in God. I'm not sure what sparked his newfound interest, but I noticed that he regularly attended my "Chap Rap" classes, which featured testimonies and live music from former gang members and dealers of his heritage. They told him he was living a lie and that the "game" was a dead-end street, which made a powerful impression on him.

Fili also began attending church services and joining our faith-based movie nights whenever we held them. We developed a good working relationship over several months. When I thought he was ready, I asked if he would like to read *The Shot Caller*. To my pleasant surprise, he said yes.

I gave him a copy of Casey's book and sat back as I allowed God to do the rest. Fili, to his credit, stayed on task and finished the book. He told me he really identified with Casey because he also had the same addiction to stabbing that Casey had. That was a telling admission that showed his heart was softening. But Fili was still not there yet.

As he continued to await sentencing, he had a conversation with a rival Nuestra Family gang member[1] who told Fili he had accepted Christ. "You need to talk to the chaplain and give your life to God, bro," the former gang member said.

When Fili and I got together for another visit, he was tearing up. "Why is this, Chap? What's happening?"

"It's the presence of the Holy Spirit," I replied. "That's what you're feeling."

Before our time wrapped up, and sensing the moment was right, I offered Fili the opportunity to receive Christ in his life.

"Yes, I'd like to do that," he whispered.

I baptized Fili full immersion in our facility, praying that the Lord would change him for the better.

On the day of his sentencing in 2019, after four years of waiting, I had three prayer warriors, one man and two women, in the courtroom, praying that justice would be served and that Fili would find favor in the courtroom. We noticed the judge stepped into his chamber multiple times for closed-door meetings with the prosecutors and defense attorneys. In the end, however, the judge overrode the district attorney's recommendation and sentenced Fili to a minimum of *nine* years with a maximum of fifteen.

Fili accepted the court's verdict humbly. Even though fellow inmates encouraged him to fight the sentence, he never did. "This is God's will," he said.

Fili sure had my back when I was dealing with Jorge. He must have told Jorge a half-dozen times that Casey's story was on the level. Fili was just as bold to married gang members in his pod, saying things like, "When you get out, you need to be a father. You need to be a better husband." He led prayer groups that became so big that the COs broke them up because they thought the inmates were meeting to discuss going after other gang members. They weren't. They were

---

1 Also known as the NF gang, the Spanish words translate to "Our Family."

hearing prayer requests and praying for each other.

Then a shot of excellent news: Fili was paroled in late 2021 for "good behavior" because he demonstrated he was a changed man. When he came out of the system, he made a request: he wanted to see the judge who sentenced him and thank him for giving him a longer prison sentence than the one recommended by the district attorney.

Why? Because without the longer sentence, he would've never received *The Shot Caller* from me—a book that changed his life and gave him the hope he could turn his life around and be a good father to his children.

Fili asked me to accompany him to the judge's chambers, which I agreed to do. The fact that the judge was willing to meet Fili in his office was risky, considering Fili's past life.

After shaking hands, Fili cleared his throat.

"Judge, I asked to see you because I want to personally thank you for the longer sentence because I would never have become a Christian. That's what I am now."

"Well, I'm impressed," the judge replied. "I certainly remember you and your case. That was a tough decision for me. I struggled because I read your record of living on the streets at ten and joining a gang to survive. But I must tell you: this is certainly a first, a former inmate thanking me for a longer sentence."

Fili's eyes shone from his tears. "I mean it," he told the judge. "I don't know where I'd be today if it weren't for Christ and all of Chap's help." That's when Fili nodded toward me.

And then it was my turn to get choked up as I watched this former gang member and a Circuit Court judge embrace each other and exchange encouraging words about God and faith.

The judge looked at his watch. "Listen, I have to get going, but you have an open invitation to have lunch with me anytime. If you need it, I'll be happy to write a letter of recommendation for getting a job or housing."

Fili remained in northeast Wisconsin for his safety because he was asked to testify against a higher-ranking shot caller in Ventura County. While in Wisconsin, he ministered in the streets, exhorting gang members to leave the lifestyle while they still had a chance to become good fathers and husbands.

It shocked me when I heard the news that Fili died in his mid-forties from a fentanyl overdose in April 2022. Going out that way made no sense for a guy on fire for the Lord. Why would he get sucked back into drugs, especially when he understood the dangers? The case is still under investigation, but I can connect the dots: Fili had to be taken out.

Fili never got to see his two children—a son and a daughter, one a teen, the other in his mid-twenties. He had stayed away from them because of his past life. He wanted to protect them.

A few months before his death, Fili had a picture taken of himself holding his Bible, dressed in his Sunday best like he was getting ready for church. He wanted to give his two children copies of the photo, but death by fentanyl got in the way.

It's a shame Fili's children never met this new creature in Christ whom God had redeemed. He expressed his love for them many times to me. But now Fili is with his Lord and Savior, and nothing makes me feel better.

✦   ✦   ✦

Finally, one more point: I can identify with Mical Pyeatt's story and the title of this book—*Ok, I Will.*

You see, the Lord put this message on my heart in 2023:

> *I want you to pick up and move near the West Texas border city of El Paso and minister to gang members and kids being abused and neglected.*

For weeks, I told the Lord, *I can't do that. How can I sell my home and furniture and move 1,500 miles to the southwest? There's no way I can do that.*

On top of those questions, I was still emotionally reeling from the last three years when the Covid-19 pandemic swept the country. Here is a list of my travails:

- I lost my part-time job at the hospital because hospitals are struggling financially.

- I had a stalker.

- I got Covid-19 pretty bad.

- My house burned down.

- I was named in three lawsuits and had to protect myself with three attorneys.

- My husband walked away from our marriage, ending a forty-one-year union that had given us two sons and seven grandchildren.

- We had a stressful divorce legal proceeding in which my husband tried to hide certain assets, and the insurance company fought us tooth and nail on what our destroyed home was worth.

- When we finally received a settlement on the house fire, the money was deposited into our attorney's legal account. Then cyberhackers stole all that money.[2]

So I've been under some severe stress since the pandemic began.

But I can look back and faithfully say that God is good and has had my back. He's been my husband and my whole life. I trust Him.

Yet God's voice was very distinct when He asked me to move to

---

2 The FBI has yet to successfully trace who the cyberhackers were.

West Texas and start all over. I'm unsure if He asked me *four times* as he did with Mical, but I eventually reached a point where I said to the Lord, *Ok, I will go.*

I resigned from my chaplain position with the Brown County Jail, trusting God to provide at a time when I'm approaching retirement age.

That's why I'm choosing not to retire but to refire and want to serve Him until He calls me home. There's no better way to go through life.

chapter six

A DIFFERENT KIND OF SHOT CALLER

by Marcus Schrader

A few years ago, I was mentoring a guy named Jamie Campbell, a native of London, England, who'd recently been released from federal prison for racketeering and various underworld activities.

I was counseling Jamie because I had recently launched Workforce Chaplains in my hometown of Indianapolis, Indiana, which provides chaplain services to businesses and organizations in the Indianapolis area. My team of chaplains and I were passionate about helping business leaders better serve their employees holistically by meeting their workers' spiritual and emotional needs. Although Jamie wasn't a corporate client, I sought opportunities to mentor a handful of people who needed someone to listen to what they were going through. Jamie, fresh out of prison and on work release, fit that desire of mine.

Jamie told me that when he was imprisoned in New York City, he got to know a celebrity in his cellblock: John A. Gotti, the son of the infamous Gambino family crime boss, John Gotti Jr.

John "Dapper Don" Gotti Jr. took control of the most powerful of New York's Five Families in the 1980s by an old-fashioned Mob method—assassinating his predecessor. Also nicknamed "Teflon Don" by the New York tabloids because of the failure of any charges to stick, Gotti Jr. was finally convicted of racketeering and five murders in 1992. He was sentenced to life in prison and never got out: the crime boss died of throat cancer in 2002 at sixty-one.

"Marcus, you have to watch the movie *Gotti*," Jamie said. "It's a fascinating look at the Mafia. His son told me that the family had an arrangement with the movie's producers: every scene had to be approved by the Gotti family because they cared about their patriarch's legacy. The actor John Travolta plays the lead role of Gotti."

Intrigued by the recommendation—and the personal connection to someone who was a good friend of John Gotti Jr.'s son—I watched the R-rated movie via YouTube with my oldest son, Andrew Schrader, who was in his early twenties. What fascinated me most was watching how the Mob works. The film was worthwhile and a decent watch.

Well, we all know how YouTube works: the algorithm started giving me all kinds of links on the right-hand side of my web page, and they all seemed to be for Mob movies: *American Gangster, Mafia Mamma, Capone, The Family,* and *American Hustle,* to name a few.

One recommendation that kept popping up was for a movie called *Shot Caller.* This was not Casey's story, which would be titled *The Shot Caller* anyway. I watched the trailer of *Shot Caller* and liked what I saw. I figured this film could give me more insight into the criminal world, which could prove helpful since I met all kinds of people in my chaplaincy work.

I knew my wife, Jennifer, wouldn't be interested in watching a gangster movie, so one evening when she was out, I cued up *Shot Caller* and settled in with a bowl of popcorn. I quickly realized that the main protagonist was Jacob Harlon, a straight-arrow family man played by Nikolaj Coster-Waldau, known for his work as Jaime Lannister on *Game of Thrones*.

The premise of *Shot Caller* goes like this: Jacob is a successful stockbroker living the white-picket-fence life in the sunny Southern California suburb of Pasadena. He is happily married to Kate, a doting father to their only child, a son, and plays pickup basketball to stay in shape. His lifestyle is the epitome of a comfortable, carefree upper-middle-class life.

One evening, Jacob and Kate go out on a dinner date with another couple. Lots of pasta and vino rosso. On their way home, Jacob is behind the wheel, yucking it up with the other couple, when tragedy strikes: Jacob runs a red light and collides with a pickup truck. His basketball buddy Tom is killed. A police investigation determines that Jacob's blood-alcohol level is .10, over the legal limit, leading the local district attorney to charge him with manslaughter.

Jacob's attorney doesn't like their chances at winning at trial since the judge assigned to the case is aggressive with DUI perps. Kate insists he fight the charges, but his attorney advises Jacob to take a plea deal and serve thirty months, which will likely drop to sixteen for good behavior. Jacob decides to accept the offer on the table, counting on keeping his head down and quietly enduring his time of incarceration. If all goes well, he can resume everyday family life in less than a year and a half.

Once inside, though, Jacob learns the reality of prison: each racial group segregates themselves. Latinos gang up with Latinos, blacks with blacks, and whites with whites. In his lockup, a white supremacist gang known as the Aryan Brotherhood warns Jacob that he won't survive as a lone wolf, but if he's willing to fall in with them and get his hands "dirty," they'll keep him safe.

Jacob is put between the proverbial rock and a hard place: if he doesn't line up these hardened, violent criminals, they'll kill him and he'll never see his wife and kid again. Even though he's unsure about which direction to go, Jacob decides he'll do what it takes to live. He helps the Aryan Brotherhood smuggle drugs into prison and takes part in the murder of another inmate. When he's implicated in the crime, the court adds another nine years to his sentence.

The transformation of Jacob Harlon is now complete. He rises in the gang and becomes a shot caller in prison. His fellow gang members nickname him "Money," an ode to his past life in the financial world.

The film moves quickly to Jacob's release date, which arrives after serving ten years in the slammer. Before he's released, he's tasked by the Aryan Brotherhood leadership to head up a gun deal with the Sureños, a Hispanic gang, after he hits the streets. He's informed that if he doesn't cooperate, well, it would be a shame if anything happened to Kate or their son. Jacob is forced to use the savage skills he learned in prison to protect the family he left behind.

While certainly not an uplifting or feel-good movie—and filled with stomach-churning violence and tons of f-bombs—I didn't feel like I wasted my time watching *Shot Caller*. I even viewed the film a second time, which confirmed that prison life was a hellhole. I joked to Jennifer that I never wanted to be locked up after seeing that movie.

As I watched *Shot Caller*, I wondered if the film's depiction of prison life in California was accurate or legit. Were there really shot callers and other cliques behind prison walls? Were the prison populations segregated by race?

These were questions I had.

CASEY

If you're wondering if I, the author of *The Shot Caller*, the book, have seen *Shot Caller*, the movie, the answer is yes.

Marcus' questions are ones I would expect from someone who's never been in or close to a prison, but before I get into those inquiries, here's my take on the film:

A lot was accurate, like how white prisoners band together inside prison, just as Latinos and blacks form their own gangs inside prison. That was true when I was behind bars, and it's still true today.

But *Shot Caller* left a distinct impression that the white supremacists were the dominant gang in numbers and strength in a California prison. Really? I did a little checking on the racial makeup of prisons in the Golden State: Hispanics make up 44 percent, blacks comprise 28 percent, and whites have 21 percent of the beds, so that was an over-the-top assumption. We have a saying in the Latino gang culture: *That's too much cream on the taco.*

Maybe groups like the Aryan Brotherhood are the top dogs in some northern-tier states with predominantly white populations, but in California, Latino gangs reign supreme, especially at Level 4 yards, because of their violence on the streets. You'd likely find more white inmates in the prison population inside the minimum-security prisons, the Level 1 yards for those who commit white-collar crimes. We called them "Camp Snoopy" since life was far easier for inmates in these country-club prisons.

Another thing that caught my attention was during visiting hours when Jacob sat behind the glass partition and looked at his forlorn wife, Kate. In one riveting scene, he broke down and cried himself a river.

As soon as I saw that, I said to myself: *That's the end of the movie.* In my world, Jacob would have been killed before the next prison chow.

Here's the deal: if you cry during visiting hours or show vulnerability by sobbing *anywhere*, your group looks weak. And shot callers can't have their groups look weak, so they would make sure they "take out the trash." Eliminate the babies who cry.

A few other things that jumped out at me:

+ The prison yard looked like it was filmed in some industrial zone and didn't come close to depicting what an actual prison yard looks like. When that scene appeared, I slapped my thigh and said, *Oh, come on.* Somebody didn't do their homework.

✦ In the movie, Jacob gets into a fight with a black prisoner. Prisoners from all races circled the two com- batants, yelling encouragement and making a ruckus as they watched them duke it out.

Here's why that scene was so unrealistic: As soon as a prisoner from one race hits another prisoner from another race today, that's an automatic race riot, no questions asked. There are no one-on-one fights in prison yards. The film director messed up royally.

✦ In a scene where Jacob was placed in his prison cell, I spotted a porcelain sink and toilet. Nope. Those fixtures are always stainless steel. At the far wall, there was a four-foot-by-four-foot window. Nope. Windows in Level 4 yards are usually two or three feet across and a few inches high, making it impossible to squeeze a body through.

On the positive side, the dialogue was somewhat accurate. Prisoners pepper their speech with four-letter words, so no surprise there.

Does that mean *Shot Caller* was a satisfactory or entertaining movie? Well, I'm sure the film was watchable to someone who has never set foot inside that system, but for someone who's been behind bars, *Shot Caller* was a disappointment. There were too many unrealistic scenarios for my taste.

MARCUS

After watching *Shot Caller*, I developed a newfound interest in prison life and discussed the film at length with Jennifer, who took notice.

A few weeks after I saw the movie, she was on YouTube and came across a video podcast called the *Becket Cook Show* in which the host and a guest discuss topics relevant to today's culture. One of Becket Cook's guests was Casey Diaz, author of *The Shot Caller,* a book about his life as a former Latino gangbanger who miraculously found God while in prison. Jennifer was transfixed by the nearly hour-long interview and thought I'd want to read the book. Father's Day was coming up, so she surprised me with this gift.

When I unwrapped my present and held the black-covered book in my hands, my first question was this: "Oh, is this based on the movie?"

"No, no, no," she replied. "It's the opposite. This is a true story of a real shot caller who got saved in prison."

I set the book aside for a month. Then one day in the summer of 2022, I picked it up. What an amazing story! Everything resonated with me.

Here's why I loved Casey's book so much: he knew he was in a tough spot when he told the gang leaders in the prison yard that he was a Christian and couldn't take part in what they were doing any longer. It's a miracle they didn't kill Casey. Usually, when you want to leave a gang, that's a death sentence. But God protected him, although he had to endure many beatings.

✦　✦　✦

Whenever I run into a friend or acquaintance and talk about what films we've seen, I'll ask them if they've seen the movie *Shot Caller* because I want to tell them about Casey's book. I'd say that probably half of American men between the ages of forty and sixty-five have seen the film or at least heard of it.

Hey, have you seen the movie Shot Caller?

If I receive an affirmative reply, I'll say, *Then you've got to read the book* The Shot Caller. *It's nothing like the movie. It's a true story of a guy who finds Christ in prison. Would you like a copy? Because I've got one.*

That's true. I keep a handful of *Shot Caller* books with me, either in my office or in my car. I've probably given away four or five dozen, ordering them five or ten at a time on Amazon. I view this as part of my ministry, which includes doing pro bono chaplaincy work for our county's drug court, overseen by a circuit court judge I've gotten to know. Many counties in my home state of Indiana provide treatment for people's addictions instead of incarcerating them. The people in drug court want to turn their lives around like Casey did, so I'll offer them a book. I even gave the county drug court judge a copy of *The Shot Caller* and placed another copy in the drug court library.

I've found *The Shot Caller* to be a great calling card whenever I visit a county prison or state penitentiary. Prisoners prefer straight talk, so I'll speak in this fashion: "This guy, Casey Diaz, liked to stab people. His preferred method was stabbing other gang members with a flathead screwdriver."

That always gets someone's attention. I've given away more books this way.

But you know what I like best about *The Shot Caller*? It's an excellent evangelistic tool for those who haven't yet given their lives to Christ. I tell these folks, "I think you would be interested in seeing how God helped this guy in a really tough situation."

I hope and pray that they'll stick with the book and get to the part where Casey sees his life played back to him on a wall in his cell. If they do, then I'm confident God will use this incredible supernatural story to lead them to Him, just like He did with Casey.

✦ ✦ ✦

Workforce Chaplains is open 24/7 and always on call. Hurting or troubled employees can call, text, or email a chaplain anytime. And they get regular visits too. It could be once a week, every other week, or even once a month.

These days, I oversee about forty chaplains serving around three dozen companies representing 35,000 employees. We primarily serve businesses in Indiana that want to provide spiritual care to their employees as a benefit. We decided early on that we would have male and female chaplains with white, black, and Latino chaplains, so we have a diverse team and pay our people well. Historically, chaplains make little, so I doubled their starting salaries. I think that's one reason the Lord's blessed us.

Our motto is to love, serve, and care for anyone and everyone. They don't have to be believers or casual churchgoers. They can be atheists; they can be whatever. That's our external mission.

Our internal mission is to make a friend, be a friend, and lead that friend to Christ. We do not lead with that since some people are not religious and companies frown on proselytizing. But when God opens the door, we can walk through that opening and bring Christ to them. We remind executives that we're there to love, serve, care, and be a friend to the company's employees.

Why do people want to talk to a chaplain provided by the company? Because it's safe for them. Our conversations are strictly confidential and not shared with their human resources department. Usually, we're contacted when the employee is fighting or going through a rough patch with a spouse or a partner, or maybe their teenager is out of control and they don't know where to turn or who to talk to.

One cool thing is that I hired a chaplain on our team because I had read Casey's book. His name is Jerry Wills, who served a thirty-six-year sentence in California for killing a guy, but it was in self-defense. The homicide happened when Jerry came home and found a guy in bed with his girlfriend. Sharp words were exchanged, a struggle ensued, and a man was shot and killed. The problem was that an off-duty police officer died with a father who was a high-ranking police officer too.

While he was held in jail without bail, awaiting trial, a prison chaplain led Jerry to the Lord. From day one in federal prison, Jerry was faithful to God after being sentenced in 1979. Jerry connected with the warden, led Bible studies for other prisoners, and completed over 100 units of correspondence Bible study courses through Southern California Bible College. Prison administrators and COs attested to his faith, integrity, work ethic, and dedication to helping people.

Jerry went in when he was in his thirties and didn't get out until he was close to seventy, but his Hoosier roots called him back to Indianapolis. He completed a Christian Chaplains & Coaches course to receive his certification as a chaplain and joined Workforce Chaplains soon after that. That he had been in for over thirty-five years didn't bother me. Casey's book has helped me be more open about hiring an ex-con and former murderer to join our team.

Unlike Jacob "Money" Harlon, prison did not change Jerry Wills. Instead, Jerry changed the prison around him—just like Casey did in *The Shot Caller.*

part 3

3

A MESSAGE OF HOPE

chapter seven

A CREW CUT

by James Diaz

'm Casey's brother, but readers of *The Shot Caller* wouldn't know Casey had a brother because he left my name out of the book. I understand why he did so: there were so many moving parts to his amazing story that he needed to strip things down. He was also eleven years older than me, meaning I was an infant when he was jumped into the Rockwood Street Locos. I was too young to factor into *The Shot Caller* story.

Nor did Casey have room to describe how my mother and I came to the Lord when I was around fifteen years old. Casey had been out of prison for just a short time—just a couple of months—when he found a cheap apartment in San Pedro, a working-class port city near the Los Angeles Harbor. He was still getting his bearings on the outside.

One weekend afternoon, Casey invited Mom and me to come over with Abel Ruiz, who'd been on the inside with Casey at New Folsom. In Casey's book, he talked about Abel, a former member of Florencia 13 who'd found Christ in prison. He led Bible studies in my brother's pod, which Casey attended and benefited from as a new Christian. Abel was one of those charismatic persons who couldn't stop talking about Jesus and loved sharing the gospel. He and Casey had grown very close in prison and were even tighter on the outside.

That afternoon, we all showed up at Casey's tiny apartment. My brother, new at this host thing, realized he had nothing to offer his guests. He asked if he could run to a nearby convenience store and pick up some tortilla chips and soft drinks.

Of course, we said yes. While my brother was gone, Abel did his thing: he started sharing Christ with us. We'd heard the same message from Casey over the years, but for some reason or another, Mom and I had never given our hearts to the Lord despite Casey's pleadings. But something clicked that afternoon while we waited for Casey to return. Abel presented the Gospel in such an attractive way that Mom and I knew we had been holding back on God and needed to give our hearts to Him.

Casey came through the front door as the three of us stood in a circle, eyes closed and hands clasping each other, saying yes to Jesus. It was an emotional moment. Mom's tears were fresh. I choked up as well.

Casey didn't say a thing as he set down a couple of paper grocery bags filled with six-packs of Coke and bags of chips. When Abel finished and our hands were released, my brother realized he had witnessed an extraordinary moment. We hugged each other, and then Casey did something typical of him: he made a wisecrack.

"Mom, I can't believe you," he said, doing a good acting job. "I've been talking to you for seven years about being born again, and this stranger comes in and you're saying yes to the Lord just like that?"

We all laughed, especially Abel, releasing the tension and joy. Of course, my brother was grateful that a fellow ex-con reached out and got us saved. Casey did the planting, and Abel did the reaping.

Now fast forward about twenty years to sometime in 2014. I was married to Mandy and had just moved to Simi Valley from Northridge.

I had started a lighting company, and we had a toddler daughter named Abby. Simi Valley was a bedroom community for larger cities in Ventura County to the west and the San Fernando Valley and LA to the south.[1] The population of 100,000 was predominantly white—80 percent—so there weren't a lot of Hispanic families in Simi Valley, but we were fine with that since everyone seemed to get along. (Mandy is white.) We continued to go to our home church in Northridge called Discovery.

One Saturday afternoon, Mandy and I dropped by our church to go over the program for the Sunday service. The elders had asked me to share my testimony with the congregation, which I was glad to do. They also wanted to hear what I would say and tell me how much time I had. When we finished the meeting, I turned to my wife.

"You think I need a haircut?" I liked to wear my hair short and combed to the side. I certainly wanted to look my Sunday best.

Mandy studied me. "Yeah, you could use a trim," she replied.

I called my regular barber in Northridge, but he was on vacation. We drove toward Simi Valley, figuring that Google Maps would help us find a barber shop. We were pressed for time because it was approaching five o'clock. Every barber shop in Simi Valley had closed, so we kept driving around aimlessly. We finally found this random barbershop in the middle of nowhere. The barbershop wasn't much to look at and didn't even have a red-and-white striped barber's pole next to the entrance.

The door was open, but the shop was empty except for four heavy-duty leather chairs anchored to green-and-white checked flooring.

"Anyone here?" I asked.

A massive dude with close-cropped blond hair stepped through a curtain. If I had to guess his age, he looked to be in his mid-thirties. His weathered face, covered with a stubble of three-day growth, sent

1 Simi Valley's claim to fame is being home to the Ronald Reagan Presidential Library, where the former president was buried in 2004.

a message: *Don't mess with me.*

"Sure, come on in," he said a bit gruffly.

I knew enough about prison life from Casey to recognize the prison tats on his neck and arms. (I had never been in prison myself.) He was an ex-con, no doubt. I figured he was one of those white supremacist dudes that Casey ran into at New Folsom, so my guard was up.

"I need a haircut," I said. "You have time?"

He looked me up and down. I wasn't sure what was going to happen.

"Take this chair," he pointed.

No sooner had I plopped my frame into his chair when he swooped in with a beige cape, which he cinched a bit too tightly around my neck. I raised my eyebrows to Mandy, who'd taken a seat and was pretending to rifle through a magazine while she kept an eye on me.

"What's a guy like you doing in Simi Valley?" he asked, reaching for his clippers.

I knew exactly what he meant: *What's a Hispanic guy like you doing in a white area like Simi Valley on a Saturday afternoon?*

I didn't take the bait—a good idea since he had a sharp instrument in his hands. I thought I could turn down the temperature in the shop by telling him the truth—that I loved living here.

"I need a trim because I'll be sharing my testimony at my church in the morning. That's why I'm here."

"So you go to church," he commented. I noticed a slight chuckle.

"Yeah," I replied.

"Well, I've got a church story."

"Tell me about it." I was curious about what would come out of his mouth.

"I was going to Real Life, a church in Santa Clarita," he began.[2] Every time I walked in, I saw the looks of people who wanted nothing to do with me. That bothered me because I was struggling with hard

---

2 Santa Clarita is twenty-five miles northwest of Simi Valley.

times. I was also questioning God and getting frustrated that nobody wanted to approach me or welcome me. I told God, 'I'm going to give You one more chance, and if nobody reaches out or says anything to me, I'm done. I'm sick and tired of no one wanting to talk to me.'"

That was understandable. The barber was a scary-looking dude. Gruff. Unapproachable. That was the vibe I got, but nobody should be treated that way.

"That's not right," I ventured. And it wasn't. But this barber was rough around the edges.

He continued clipping as he picked up his story.

"When I yelled at God that Saturday night, I said to Him, 'If You don't make something different happen in Your church tomorrow, I'll never go back to one of Your churches again.' I meant what I said, 100 percent.

"The following morning, I walked into the sanctuary and approached one of the front rows. I guess I wanted people to see me, to notice I was there. Once again, no one attempted to introduce themselves or say hello to me.

"We went through the worship songs, and all that was good, and then the pastor got up to deliver his sermon. The message that morning was on second chances and that God was in the business of changing lives, every one of us, even those who had been imprisoned. That got my attention. Then the pastor said, 'We shot a video recently with a former gangbanger whose life dramatically changed when he was incarcerated. I want you to see this.'

"The sanctuary darkened. On a gigantic video screen, I saw the pastor interviewing this Hispanic guy. He talked about how he grew up in the LA gangs and was busted for murdering someone. He said he was so notorious for being a gang leader that the prison authorities put him in solitary confinement, and that's where he found Jesus. I'm telling you, his testimony really hit me. He didn't hold back about who he was in the gang world before God saved him.

"But while watching this video, I told myself, *I'm not as bad as he was. If God could do something for that guy, maybe He could do something for me.*

"When the service was over, I went to the front and talked to one of the other pastors. I said I wanted to get right with Jesus after that gangbanger's testimony. The pastor said, 'Great!' He explained the gospel and led me to the Lord. I believed that He died for my sins so that I could have eternal life with Him. When I finished praying, the pastor was emotional and warmly hugged me. Others saw what had happened and came over to greet me. For the first time in that church, I felt welcomed."

The barber's story touched me, but I wondered who the gangbanger was. His story sounded vaguely like my brother's testimony.

"My brother came from the gangs too," I ventured. "He got saved in prison."

"Oh, yeah, man. This guy was the real deal. He said he was a high-up shot caller."

A shot caller. A shiver ran down my spine. "Do you remember his name?"

"Yeah. Casey Diaz."

"Dude, that's my brother."

The barber stopped clipping. "I don't believe you."

"Here, let me show you."

I reached into my pocket for my phone and quickly found a shot of Casey. "Is that him?"

The white dude gasped. "Yes, it is!"

He started sobbing right before Mandy and me—because what were the odds? As soon as I stood out of my barber's chair, the barber wrapped me in his arms and wept and wept. He couldn't believe that I was the brother of the guy on the video who changed his life.

What a faith-affirming moment for him and me. Together, we experienced a divine moment.

CASEY

When James got that haircut in Simi Valley, Mical and I had been working for nearly two years to get my story out there, but we had nothing to show for our efforts. Mical has already shared how his marriage was in tatters and how he was in the middle of an ugly custody fight. My family situation was just as brutal. Sana and I were financially at rock bottom. We were getting hit from all sides. Everything was down the toilet. We needed some oxygen—a lift.

That Saturday night, Mical and I were sitting around my kitchen table, feeling whipped and depressed from everything happening to us since the day Mical said to the Lord, *Ok, I will.*

When James called to tell us what happened, Mical and I listened with excitement, thinking the entire time: *God is good.* Hearing my brother's story at that exact moment was like eating protein for the first time in six months.

Re-energized, we pushed on.

chapter eight

CAMP MILLER

by Erasmo "Raz" Reyes

'm a fan of *The Shot Caller* because Casey and I have a lot in common:

- + we were both born in 1972
- + we both grew up in the Los Angeles area
- + we were both jumped into gangs when we were eleven
- + we were both arrested at fifteen and slept in the same dorm at Camp Miller, a juvenile detention facility
- + we both came to the Lord in prison
- + we're great friends today and look out for each other

There are, however, some significant but subtle differences that readers will find interesting as I share my story.

+ + +

I grew up in Van Nuys in the San Fernando Valley, a flat basin becoming increasingly multiracial in the late 1970s and 1980s. I didn't know Casey since he was fifteen miles south of me in Koreatown near downtown LA.

Casey was the son of El Salvador immigrants who entered this country legally, but that wasn't my situation. My parents came to the US illegally from a town outside Guadalajara in Central Mexico. My father, Erasmo Reyes, shared the same last name as my mother, Catalina Reyes, but they never married after I was born at Valley Presbyterian Hospital in Van Nuys. Maybe that made filling out my birth certificate easier, but my father was never in the picture. He abandoned my mother and me shortly after my birth, and I had no real relationship with him growing up. Maybe he'd drop by every six months, but that was it.

Mom and I lived in a one-bedroom apartment with my grandmother and aunts and uncles, crammed in like sardines. There were usually between eight to twelve people sleeping there every night, and here's how we managed that. All the women slept in the single bedroom with two bunk beds and a twin bed, so five could fit. In the living room, a king-sized bed took up most of the room, along with two couches. For the guys and me, it was "Musical Chairs": when the lights went out, whoever got a spot got a decent place to sleep. Otherwise, you were sleeping on the floor.

With no help from my absent father, my mother worked two jobs to keep us fed and clothed. Her day job was at Mission Linen Supply, which supplied linens and uniforms to hospitals, medical offices, restaurants, etc. Then at five o'clock, she put in four or five hours as a janitor at the Valley School, an elite K-8 private school in Van Nuys. Sometimes she had me help her out, but I think she brought me along so she would know where I was. I grew up as an unsupervised kid on the streets, used to doing whatever I wanted.

We lived on Delano Street, a Hispanic neighborhood that was a hodgepodge of small, cheaply built apartment buildings and shady bungalows surrounded by orange trees. I walked a mile to Chandler Elementary, just over the boundary line in Sherman Oaks, an LA suburb of 100,000 that was *far* different from Van Nuys. Sherman Oaks was a rich white area with a lot of Jewish families. Three-fourths of Chandler Elementary was white, and the rest were Hispanic, like myself.

During my six years at Chandler Elementary, I was never invited to a birthday party by any white kids or invited to their homes after school. My English was fluent with barely an accent, so that wasn't an issue.[1]

It's like we led separate lives. In many ways, we did.

✦ ✦ ✦

In the fourth, fifth, and sixth grades, I was an honors student, one of those quick learners who constantly bugged the teacher with questions. But once the school bell sounded and I crossed Burbank Boulevard into Van Nuys, I was literally back on the streets.

When I walked with classmates, anything could happen. My buddies and I were always up to something. If we weren't up to something, we were up to no good, like entering Maloney Stationers, a Hallmark-like store, and stealing stickers, pens, crayons, and erasers. I probably started stealing when I was in the first grade. Swiping stuff became a very ordinary—even fun—thing to do. If we weren't grabbing and walking off with stuff that wasn't ours, we were into all kinds of mischief.

When I was an eleven-year-old fifth grader, I was sitting in class when one of my friends sent me a note. His name was Shadow.

The note said:

> *I'm going to start a clique from the neighborhood. If you want in, meet me at the park after school.*

A clique is a subset of a gang.

---

1 My mother tongue is Spanish, which I spoke at home with Mamacita and my relatives.

So why would a bunch of eleven-year-old boys want to start their own clique? It's because we looked up to Barrio Van Nuys (BVN), the largest gang in Van Nuys, and we wanted to be like them. Boys my age were trying to figure out who we were and where we fit in the world.

Starting our own mini-gang was a way to provide a sense of belonging and acceptance that we weren't getting anywhere. It would also give us a sense of protection from bullies and other forms of violence. Since my homeboys Shadow, Creepy, Morro, Bothe, and I were shrimps, we paid homage to BVN by calling ourselves the Barrio Van Nuys Pequenos, or "little ones."

Many people don't know that Mexican gangs don't have leaders per se. Everyone is kind of equal, but we all know that nobody's equal in the long run. There are high achievers in life, dudes who are more influential than others, whether it's because of grit or high IQ. But the gang code says that a gang member can't say, "I'm that guy," and tell others what to do. But he can lead by example and influence others. Being a doer is a form of leadership that others gravitate to.

That description fit me: while I wasn't the self-appointed leader of our BVN clique, I had a lot of input on what we were going to do, like getting into rumbles or stealing cans of spray paint from Builder's Emporium so we could go on a "writing" spree—tagging. We were so ahead of our peers that the BVN Pequenos became an overnight sensation.

No one from Barrio Van Nuys—homies in their mid-to-late teens and early twenties—gave us any advice or tried to steer us in a particular direction. But we were paying close attention to how they dressed and behaved.

And what guns they packed.

✦ ✦ ✦

I got my first gun in seventh grade when I started attending Van Nuys Junior High, where the school population was half-white and half-Hispanic. Inside this racially tinged tinderbox, a lot of Star Model S

.380 pistols floated around. I picked one up off the street.

I needed a gun because the BVN Pequenos were moving drugs, and when drugs are sold, shootings and homicides weren't far behind.

In my junior high years, I started getting arrested by the LAPD, usually for shootings or fighting in school. The police gang unit opened a file on me. I was a Top 10 gang member by the time I was fourteen. If I were an athlete, I would have been known as a blue chipper, but I wasn't a quarterback who threw long touchdown passes or made the three-point shot from long range on the basketball court. I was full-on into the gang life, much like Casey was at that age.

Because of my advanced skills on the street, I caught the eye of a twenty-five-year-old gangbanger named Loco, a member of Barrio Van Nuys. He was an athletic guy, good-looking, and six feet, two inches—tall for a Mexican. He set the pace in the 'hood and committed a ton of robberies. Loco was kind of a talent scout, looking to see who was coming up, who was in the pipeline. He took a liking to me.

This guy has a lot of potential, he told others. *Raz is really good at what he's doing. He's a standout.*

When those compliments reached my ears, I stood taller. Walked with more spring in my step. I liked how Loco embraced me. He would pick me up, drive me around, and buy me clothes. Because I was running with one of the top guys running Van Nuys, that put me in a different category than everyone else, which meant I needed to upgrade to a Ruger LCR 9mm revolver—perfect for daily carry. When dealing drugs, one needed a small, lightweight gun if a deal went south.

✦ ✦ ✦

As a freshman, I started attending North Hollywood High and had a girlfriend who lived on Valerio Street at the very north end of Van Nuys. Since I was spending a lot of time in that neighborhood, which the Valerio Street Locos ran, I had to be careful. BVN Pequenos had a reputation, so we were targets.

One of my homies also had a girlfriend on Valerio Street. He was visiting her at her apartment when he was tipped off that gang members from the Valerio Street Locos were waiting for him.

He called me. "Hey, Raz. These guys from Valerio Street are up to no good. They want to jump me."

I gathered several other Pequenos and drove over to Valerio Street. When we exited the car, Valerio Street hoods opened fire on us. The high-pitched noise of bullets traveling through the air was unmistakable: we were under attack. Car windows exploded into bits of glass chards. We scattered along the sidewalk, but while hustling to hide behind a car, I felt a searing pain on the left side of my abdomen. I fell to the ground, knowing immediately that I'd been hit.

As the seconds passed, I went into shock as the two gangs reloaded and fired more bullets. Chaos and commotion reigned as one of my buddies dragged me to safety behind a car. My body tingled because I felt hot.

I noticed my red blood spilling on the sidewalk. I was dying. I sensed this was the end, which created all sorts of emotions I had trouble understanding. Was my life going to be over at the age of fifteen? It sure seemed like it.

When we heard police sirens in the distance, the shooting stopped. I had nearly passed out when I was loaded into a friend's car for the trip to the emergency room at a Kaiser hospital in nearby Panorama City.

"Am I going to die?" I asked one of my homies as the car sped along Roscoe Boulevard.

"Hold on, Raz! We're going to get you there," he responded.

I later learned from my doctors that I nearly died on the operating table. There was a lot of internal bleeding. The bullet eviscerated my left kidney, which had to be removed. I survived and would spend the next two weeks recuperating in the hospital, thinking dark thoughts about exacting revenge.

It was probably another month before I felt like my old sense:

confident, cocky, and collected. But physically, I was struggling. An infection caused whitish-yellow gobs of pus to drain from my incision, which looked gross and smelled horrible. A nurse trained my mother to clean my incision and change the gauze on my stomach, which looked like I was wearing a Pamper diaper.

I knew I was vulnerable when I returned to North Hollywood High. I remained wary of others and my surroundings. If someone knocked me down and kicked me in the stomach, I could die because I had some sort of deficiency in my blood.

I remember fifth-period PE. Even before the shooting, I never suited up and joined the lines of those doing jumping jacks or running the mile. Instead of the PE teachers disciplining me or making me run *two* miles, I was told to sit on a bench for the entire class hour. The school administration knew the score: I was a gang member leading an entirely different life. Their attitude was: *Let's go through the motions and appease him. This dude is on a whole different level than the other problem students.*

In other words, they didn't want to deal with me.

One day, I bumped into an 18ᵗʰ Street gang member inside the locker room. From the look in his eyes, I knew he had it out for me. Words were exchanged, but no one threw the first punch. When he sat down on the bench to change into gym clothes, a fight-or-flight instinct came over me. While he bent over to undo his shoelaces, I kicked him in the face as hard as possible with my hobnail boots. An uppercut busted his nose.

The dude screamed, and blood spurted everywhere. A PE teacher ran over immediately. He freaked out as well, asking me what the hell I was doing.

I wasn't too bothered by my actions. My attitude was, *Hey, that's what he gets.*

The assault resulted in my arrest and being sent to Camp Miller, a juvenile detention center tucked away in the rugged foothills between the San Fernando Valley and Malibu on the coast. One of the kids in my dorm was fifteen years old, small in stature but built like a fire hydrant. I learned quickly that you didn't mess with him.

His name was Casey Diaz.

✦　✦　✦

Casey was with Rockwood Street Locos, whose turf was near downtown LA. Even though there were probably hundreds of gang cliques in Los Angeles County, I had heard of Rockwood Street because of their unique writing style. They were setting precedents for the distinctive way they tagged buildings and signs. Everyone would try to emulate, copy, and adapt their lettering, which was a class by itself.

We had to go to classes at Camp Miller, where I noticed Casey writing in his notebook. Even from a distance, I could see he had distinctive gang-like writing, but I didn't like him. Why? Because the person who shared his bunk—his "bunkie"—was a dude named Elfie. He was from 18th Street. Those guys were our archrivals, so any friend of Elfie was an enemy of mine.

Eventually, Casey and Elfie started wolfing on me in the dorm. With my short fuse lit, I vaulted into both with my fists, which earned me time in "the box," which we called solitary confinement. By the time I got out, Casey had been released.

I spent about nine months at Camp Miller before being handed my release papers. I moved back in with Mom and went straight back to the streets. I got even more immersed in gang life and did horrible things, including shooting and paralyzing a rival from another gang. That happened when I was eighteen. I was arrested, tried as an adult, and sent to Donavan State Prison, a medium-security prison near the Mexican border.

There was a lot of turmoil in that lockup. We had a mix of Mafia types, Northern Mexicans, and African American inmates, so when we were out in the yard, you could bank on a fight breaking out. There were so many brawls that the correctional officers (COs) started betting on which inmate would get the best of it—who had more dog in him. For them, it was fun and games, but for us, it was often life and death, especially if the armed guards overlooking the yard began firing to quell the riot in the yard.[2]

I don't know if I was a betting favorite among the COs, but I was at the peak of my physical ability at five feet, eleven inches and 180 pounds of muscle honed by burpees and pushups.[3] This is partially why I wasn't displeased when I was removed from the general population for my gang status and placed in the Security Housing Unit, or the SHU. Solitary confinement may have saved my life.

✦ ✦ ✦

Throughout my twenties, I was in and out of prison, traveling on a fast route to nowhere. I was twenty-nine when I found myself at a supermax state prison in Tehachapi, thirty-five miles east of Bakersfield in the high desert.

I was questioning what I was doing because my life sucked, so you can say I was searching. To pass the time, I enjoyed reading the *Chicken Soup for the Soul* books, which featured short, inspirational stories and motivational essays. They often hinted at spirituality, but I knew nothing about God. If I didn't understand certain words, I had a dictionary to look them up. I didn't want to be known as a dumb gang member. I always read and studied different things because I wanted to be able to hold a conversation with anybody.

One of the prisoners I liked conversing with was Fernando (not his real name), a couple of cells over. He was a Mexican national and a very sharp guy.

Fernando tried to minister to me, but I didn't like hearing it. He

---

2 The feds got wind of this handicapping of prisoners, if you will, and launched an investigation that resulted in the arrest of numerous COs.

3 No pumping iron at Donovan, where weights would have been too dangerous to put out for the prison population, so we did body-weight exercises.

kept trying to give me the gospel, but I would refute him by saying things like, "How do you know God exists?" But Fernando was so engaging, so smart, that I looked forward to our conversations. Although he planted and watered many seeds, I did not come to Christ.

I had a girlfriend while I was doing time at Tehachapi. Her name was Patricia, or Patty, nine years younger than me and Hispanic. I'd met her on the street when she was hanging out with my homeboy's wives. I was attracted to her, but she didn't want anything to do with me. I kept pursuing her, even after I got sent back to prison. I'd regularly write her letters.

She would come to visit me on Sundays, Visiting Day, which kept me going. One time, she told me that she could no longer come.

"Why's that?" I inquired.

"Because that's when I go to church. I've become a Christian."

I didn't like hearing that. I tried to manipulate my girlfriend to change her mind, but she stood firm.

Fernando explained why Patty wasn't coming to see me on Sundays. "You know what?" he began. "If you want to interfere with God, God will remove her from your life. So if you love her like you say you do, just let her go to church on Sunday 'cause you won't win that battle."

I had no visitors for four months, which just about killed me. She had given me a Bible, so I started reading out of boredom or feeling I had nothing better to do. I didn't want anyone to see me reading the Bible, though, because I didn't want people to think I was weak. But God's Word touched me. I was supposed to be some kind of tough guy, but I would think, *Man, what the heck's going on with you?* On more than a few occasions, I'd be close to tears.

I began not to care about gang life anymore. I had this overwhelming desire to change and be different, but I didn't know how to get out.

One Sunday, with no visitors coming to see me, I decided to go to the church service inside the prison. An ex-gang member named

Bobby McConnell preached a sermon on the Prodigal Son, precisely what I needed to hear. I was that Prodigal Son who had squandered everything but would be welcomed into Jesus' arms.

The invitation was given, and I went forward and prayed to receive Christ in my heart. I instantly gave up everything from my past life.

When I was released about six months later, I walked out of that prison in Tehachapi and was greeted by Patty. Within a couple of months, we were married.

I started working at Roadside Lumber in Agoura Hills, where I got to know the regulars—the general contractors who dropped by to pick up 2x4s, plywood sheets, and plumbing supplies. They all seemed to be doing well for themselves with their shiny new trucks, so I thought there was a future there. When I mentioned my desire to learn the trade to one of the general contractors, he offered to take me on.

I pounded nails and hung drywall for four years and studied for my general contractor's license, which I passed.

Around 2008, I got a call from someone who wanted me to renovate a townhome he and his wife had purchased in Sylmar, part of the San Fernando Valley. Said his name was James Diaz.

Diaz is a common last name in the Mexican culture, so I didn't connect him to Casey until we started discussing our past and learning how much we had in common. I was excited to hear Casey's testimony and that he'd become a pastor at a church in Burbank while running his sign shop.

I visited Casey at his sign shop to talk about how good God is and how He rescued us. People don't realize that the late 1980s was a very dangerous time to be a gang member in Los Angeles. That period was incredibly violent, even sociopathic. You could lose your life in a heartbeat.

Yet God was and is so good to both of us. Now that we are older, we are sounding boards for each other—and brothers in the Lord.

CASEY

I loved how God reconnected Raz and me, but I have a different memory of how we met at Camp Miller when we were fifteen-year-old teens. Maybe we were hit too many times on the head.

I was there before Raz arrived, so he is correct there. I'll never forget when he walked into our dorm carrying a blanket and a fish kit.[4] Everyone knew he was the new guy.

About 120 kids, all gang members, were housed in our dorm. The bunk I shared with Elfie was one of the first Raz walked past. I'd never met the dude, but Elfie had.

"Oh, @#$%," he cussed. "My enemy just walked in here, so I'm going to have to get down with him."

Meaning, of course, that Elfie had to fight this new guy since there was still bad blood between their gangs.

"Dude, aren't you getting released Friday?" I asked.

If Elfie touched off a brawl, his release date would be pushed back.

My bunkie nodded while he kept his eyes locked on his adversary as he passed. "It is what it is," he said.

"Dude, you don't want to worry about that. I'll jam him up for you."

"Nah, you don't have to do that for me. Raz is my enemy, so I need to take care of business."

"Nope. You got to go home, brother. I'll jam him up."

The next time Raz walked past our bunk, I hopped a little cinder-block wall to get to him and started swinging. He didn't hesitate to swing back. Punches were landed, but they were more glancing blows. We clinched and kept pummeling each other until the COs ran up and separated us.

We were both sent to the box, but solitary wasn't done at Camp Miller. Those who had to do solitary confinement were frog-marched

---

4 A "fish kit" is prison slang for a bag of toiletries, such as a toothbrush, toothpaste, soap, and deodorant, given to new prisoners.

to next-door Camp Kilpatrick and locked up in one-man cells inside a U-shaped building.

All day long, we had to sit on the edge of our bed; that was our punishment. We could not lay down for a nap but had to maintain a sitting position on the edge of our bunk. The only time we were allowed to lie down was at night. Periodically, we could stand and stretch inside our locked cells.

My metal door had a window-like opening that looked out into a communal pod area. Each door was locked 24/7 except for meal and exercise times. I remember the first day when I looked through the window and spotted Raz on the other side of the U. Our eyes met, which wasn't good. We both felt there was unfinished business.

During chow time, the kitchen staff wheeled in a cart with covered plates of food or sack lunches into the middle of the pod. The cells were unlocked, and we were allowed to pick up our food and return to our perches on our bunks.

Shortly after arriving at Camp Kilpatrick, I told Raz from my cell, "The second this door opens and your door opens, it's crackin'."

"Bring it on," he replied with equal bravado.

At our next chow, we charged each other like raging bulls after our gates swung open. The COs broke up the fight with stern warnings not to engage in this type of behavior again.

I think that command lasted twenty-four hours. Our feeling was: What could they do to punish us further? Since it wasn't much, prison authorities decided to keep one of our gates locked until the other inmate picked up his food and returned to his cell, which was promptly locked.

We eventually served our time and returned to Camp Miller. You could say we learned our lesson. Or maybe we mellowed. But tension ramped up the day when one of my Rockwood homies pulled me aside. His nickname was Rat, short for Ratón, which is Spanish for *mouse*.

"Raz is a good dude, man. Cut him some slack," Rat said.

And that's how Raz and I ended up becoming friendly to each other at Camp Miller. The authorities noticed the shift in attitude and assigned us to the laundry room, where we worked well together.

Just before Raz was released, he pulled me aside. "Hey, man. I want to hit this place up," he said, meaning he wanted to gang-write all over the laundry room and leave his mark.

Raz got his hands on permanent markers and went to town, tagging the laundry room pretty good. Somehow, he got away with it.

We didn't see each other after our stints at Camp Miller, but here's the thing about gang life: you hear through the grapevine about where people are doing time in the prison system. In Raz's situation, I heard he was at Pelican Bay and Tehachapi because I had Rockwood homies there.

I got released before him, a new man in Christ. I lost track of him and his whereabouts until—and I don't believe this is a coincidence—he was hired by my brother to fix up his townhome. When Raz tried to witness to him, my brother said, "Thanks for sharing, but we're also Christians. But I had a brother who did time. He was from LA."

"Do you know what gang your brother was in?" Raz asked.

"Yeah. My brother was in Rockwood."

"Oh, I knew many of the homeboys from Rockwood and one of the bigger heads there. So who's your brother?"

"Casey."

Raz's jaw dropped to the floor. "Is Casey Diaz your brother?"

"Yeah, man."

James and Raz were so happy to discover the connection that they immediately called me on James' cell phone.

"I have someone who wants to talk to you," James said.

"Sure," I replied, none the wiser.

"What's up, Big Casey?"

"Who's this?"

"Raz Reyes. I'm sure you don't—"

I stopped him there. I knew exactly who I was talking to and told Raz that. I wondered if he had come to Christ, but he beat me to the punch and broadcast his dependence on the Lord this time.

"Praise God that He brought us back together," Raz replied. "James tells me you're a strong believer now and will ask anyone you meet if they know the Lord."

"God's been very good to me," I conceded.

I told Raz that he had to drop by my sign shop whenever he wanted so we could hang out. He's been faithful to stay in touch. Each time we see each other, all Raz and I have to do is look at each other, and we're both reminded that God intervened in our lives.

How else to explain what can't be explained, which is the mercy of a tender, loving God?

chapter nine

FINDING A HOME WITH GOD
by Franko Besinaiz

I met Casey's co-author, Mike Yorkey, at a Souly Business men's retreat in the mountains between Los Angeles and the Central Valley known as the Grapevine. He gave me a copy of *The Shot Caller,* which I devoured. I hope to meet Casey someday and tell him he's a trailblazer who paved the way for ex-gang members like me to share my past.

Because we all have a story, right?

Mine starts on my third birthday, riding in the back of a station wagon with my parents, John and Carolyn Besinaiz. I was the youngest of four children living in Fresno, the agricultural heart of California's breadbasket. We were another poor family from Mexico, having migrated up through Texas, Arizona, and California. My father was a mechanic with prominent scars on his hands, either from working on engine blocks or hitting my mother or one of us kids with a clenched fist when we did something he didn't like.

My father and mother had piled us into the family station wagon to drive us to K-Mart so they could buy me a toy gun for my birthday. I was so excited! On the ride home, I pointed the pistol and pulled the trigger at everyone and everything. Each time I fired a shot, the toy gun made a loud noise that irritated my father.

"Stop it!" he yelled from behind the wheel. His body tensed, and then he pressed the accelerator to the floor. We sped up quickly, which scared me—and Mom. My father drove like a maniac, weaving in and out of lanes, cutting off drivers, honking his horn, and tailgating to where I thought we would touch bumpers with the car in front of us.

None of us wore seat belts. Why would we?

I was standing in the front seat with my parents. My two older sisters, Christina and Yolanda, and my brother Michael sat behind us in the bench seat. Each time I snapped the trigger and made an annoying noise, my father shouted, "Stop doing that!" His outbursts revealed his growing frustration.

I quit playing with my toy gun for a bit, but then I had an idea. I leaned forward and pressed the tip of the pistol against the side of my father's head. Pulling the trigger and making that irritating noise again turned out to be a dumb idea.

My father backhanded me so hard that I flew to the rear bench and landed in my sister's laps. Now it was my turn to scream at the top of my lungs.

The station wagon was pure bedlam for twenty minutes until we arrived home. My father was pissed, my mother was pissed, and my siblings and I were upset to see them arguing and gesturing menacingly at each other.

Upon arrival, Mom sprinted into our tiny house rental. She threw some clothes in a couple of suitcases, and the next thing I knew, my mother was telling my siblings and me to get into her car.

Off we went. I was crying up a storm—not because we were leaving my father, but because I left my toy gun in his car.

✦ ✦ ✦

We eventually moved into an old, rundown house across the street from Mountain View Cemetery, one of Fresno's oldest graveyards.

Our place was so rustic that we didn't have a bathroom, so Mom had us use a weird-shaped pot in the living room. If one of us had to go No. 2, we sat on the pot right in front of everyone, and let it go. Mom or one of my sisters dumped the contents into a hole in the backyard that my mother had dug.

I pretty much was on my own growing up. I certainly didn't have anybody looking after me. If Mom wasn't working, she was on drugs half the time. I figured she didn't care about me. I spent a lot of time at the cemetery, usually at night when things were spooky and no one would see me knocking down tombstones, pulling out flowers, or destroying bouquets left behind for a loved one. I was a destructive kid.

We were hiding from my father. My mother would remind us how bad he was because of the physical beatings he gave us. We eventually moved into a garage at my grandmother's house. No bathroom there either, but at least we could use the toilet inside the main house. From there, we moved into low-income housing in Fresno—the projects. Half the time, though, we didn't have power because Mom couldn't pay the electric bill. We'd use a flashlight to see at night. If we happened to go into our bedroom and turn on the flashlight, hundreds of roaches would scatter. I never felt right sleeping in my bed. I had nightmares that roaches would nibble on my toes.

Food was scarce. Most of the time, there was nothing to eat in the cupboards or refrigerator, not even cereal and milk. I figured out a way to eat at the elementary school.[1] When the lunch bell rang, I'd stand beside the main trash can near the cafeteria with Otis, my black

---

1 This would have been in the 1970s, before the advent of school lunch programs for low-income students.

friend. He was hungry too.

Then we'd wait for classmates to give us their leftovers—half-eaten plates of spaghetti, mashed potatoes, and bits of burritos, hot dogs, and hamburgers. Dessert was Pop-Tarts, which were the best.

Every kid at my school knew this: *Don't throw away your food.* Otis and I would stack up the leftovers and eat like it was our only meal of the day—which it was.

✦ ✦ ✦

I was in third or fourth grade when two gang members got into an argument over a motorcycle. This was in the parking lot at the projects.

One was named Vito, who wanted to take Jose's motorcycle for a spin, but Jose was having none of it. They called each other names and issued threats. When Vito stepped away, it looked like things would blow over.

I was standing in front of Jose, who was talking to another gang member. Out of the corner of my eye, I saw Vito walk calmly to his car—a canary-yellow Chevy Impala with a black top—and pull out a sawed-off shotgun from the front seat.

Jose was talking with a homie and never saw or heard Vito's approach. In a flash, Vito lifted the short-barreled shotgun, placed it behind Jose's head, and squeezed the trigger. Jose's face exploded into a thousand bits. Particles of brain and flecks of blood covered my face as Jose tumbled to the ground.

My brother Michael heard the gunshot, ran to my side, grabbed my hand, and said, "We got to get out of here."

I'll never forget the sound of the shotgun blast or being sprayed with brain tissue. What happened that day traumatized me and opened the door to evilness and rage that would consume me.

✦ ✦ ✦

Not long after that, I was part of the Rabbit Foot Club. Our favorite activity was digging three- or four-foot-deep holes in a nearby field and calling them our "taverns." We'd pretend these were our homes and use our imagination to have fun.

Several kids thought it would be funny to catch me in my tavern and cover my hole with a plywood sheet to see how I reacted to being "locked up."

Suddenly, my world went dark. When I pushed back against the plywood, too many of them were on top of me to free myself, which enraged me. They continued jumping up and down on the plywood, laughing and sharing taunts. The dirt was caving in and burying me, making me even angrier. I was choking on dirt.

With all my strength, I pushed the plywood away and hopped out of the hole. Dust and grime covered my face like I was a chimney sweep, which prompted more chortling and giggles. I narrowed my eyes at one of my rivals and sprinted toward him, arms extended so I could snap his neck. I was so angry that I was looking at him through a screen of red. When he stumbled, I had an opening. I reached for a dried-up Christmas tree and threw it at him, striking him in the back. Then I beat him up badly, blow after blow with my fists. No one dared to stop me.

After that incident, I started fighting the entire neighborhood. One time, outside a convenience store, I got into it with a kid on a bike. To gain an advantage, I took a long metal stake and knocked him off his two-wheeler. Then I swung and struck him a few times, then turned my energy on his bike, banging it with the metal stake.

Whenever someone crossed me or I got into trouble, I would be transported into this red state of mind and completely lose it. I broke my teacher's arm one time because she was trying to hold me down from fighting a classmate. My anger was uncontrollable. Sometimes I tried running away when I was consumed with rage, thinking that if I made myself tired, I wouldn't be mad anymore.

But that didn't work very often.

✦   ✦   ✦

Like Casey and Raz, I started hanging out with a gang when I was eleven. My homies and I would walk through downtown Fresno and go "window-shopping." If we saw something we wanted, we would bust the window, grab what we wanted, and make a run for it. These smash-and-grabs eventually got me arrested. Very serious charges were pressed against me.

Juvenile Hall authorities judged me to be so difficult or dangerous that they wouldn't put me in a dorm room with other youthful offenders. They placed me in a single cell, which was mentally challenging to deal with.

I was given a court date for arraignment, but the court kept postponing my date because they couldn't find my mom. Meanwhile, I was remanded to custody and kept in my cell for an *entire year* until authorities finally located my mother in . . . Bakersfield, 130 miles to the south.

The judge was eager to wash his hands of me. He ordered that I be sent to Bakersfield and go before a judge there. To make sure I arrived in Bakersfield, my probation officer *and* a uniformed police officer accompanied me on a regular Greyhound bus to Bakersfield. I was placed in handcuffs for the trip. When I boarded the commercial bus, I heard someone say from the back, "Frankie, Frankie, back here."

My jaw hit the floor when I spotted my sister Yolanda. This changed everything because I was going to figure out how to get off this bus until I saw her.

When we arrived in Bakersfield, I met my mom. She was caring and loving. She wasn't high. Eventually, the court system released me with a stern warning not to come back through the juvenile system again.

I returned to school, but it wouldn't take long for word to get out that I was a Norteño—from a Northern California gang. Bakersfield was run by Sureños, or southern gangs, which meant bad blood between us.

I was part of many fights in the schoolyard and must have gotten thrown out of a half-dozen schools. One principal told me, "I don't know who you are or where you came from, but I've got to get you out of here." And off I'd go to my next school.

When I turned fourteen, I noticed Mom was returning to her old habits—doing drugs again. She wasn't around much.

One day, I came home from school to the small apartment complex we were living in. The front door was locked. We never locked our doors.

I hopped a fence and went around to the back entrance. A sliding door was locked, but the curtain was pulled back a foot. When I looked inside, our apartment looked empty. Our furniture was gone.

I went to the apartment next door and knocked. The woman who lived there was a friend of my mother's.

"Have you seen my mom?"

"Yeah, I have," she replied. "She had a U-Haul truck here today."

And then the color in the woman's face drained as she realized what had happened. "But I'm sure she's going to come back and get you," she said with a wan smile.

You don't know my mom, I thought.

There was a church next door. That night, I slept on a concrete corridor next to the sanctuary and woke up in the morning to see if Mom had returned.

She didn't, of course.

I did this for seven days, waiting for my mother to appear. I didn't eat because I had no food. Delirious from hunger, I told myself I needed to find something to eat. There was a 7-Eleven down the street with a dumpster in the back. Maybe I could scrounge something from the trash bin.

I lifted the plastic lid and looked inside the dumpster. There they were—chili dogs, still in their wrappers. I didn't care if they were hot or cold. I dove into the dumpster, closed the cover so no one could see me, and wolfed down one chili dog after another. They were warm enough.

Suddenly, the dumpster lid flew open. A lady in a 7-Eleven collared shirt was about to throw another bag of trash into the bin when she spotted me. I don't know who was more startled—her or me. I stood up, jumped out, and started running, feeling like the lowest scum of the earth. I was no better than a rat, eating leftover food in a trash bin.

I slept next to the church that night and returned to the 7-Eleven in the morning—because I was hungry. I spotted something on top of the dumpster: a box of chili dogs and a soft drink with a straw. I knew who left the food out for me—the 7-Eleven lady.

She would feed me leftover and expired food for the next two years because I was homeless, entirely on my own. There were leftover chili dogs, mini tacos, pizza slices, and a soft drink waiting for me each day.

I found a better place to sleep than the church corridor. There was an apartment complex nearby with carports in the parking lot. The carports had storage compartments that tenants could use to store stuff. I found an unlocked one big enough to hold a chaise lounge from the pool. This became my bed. I slept in the overhead compartment and could hear the school bells ring in the morning.

I was still going to school—maybe not all the time, but enough. P.E. showers are how I bathed. If I didn't attend class, I'd find a public restroom and splash water on my face and armpits.

What about clothes? I would enter a laundromat and hang out. If I saw a mom put a load of washed jeans, shirts, gym shorts, and boxers in the dryer and leave, I'd wait until the coast was clear and grab what I needed.

✦   ✦   ✦

Throughout my teen years, I worked construction on the side. I rode a bike to my jobs, where I dug ditches, hauled lumber, and pounded nails. Most of my earnings—I was always paid in cash—went to buying drugs. Contractors couldn't count on me to show up, which earned me the nickname, "No Show Franko."

Given such a nomadic life, I was still homeless at nineteen.

FINDING A HOME WITH GOD

Desperate and down. I heard voices in my head telling me, *Nobody loves you. Nobody cares about you. Just end your life.*

So that's what I decided to do.

It was a Friday night. I thought I'd dart in front of a fast-moving car, and that would be it. The busiest street was a few blocks away, so I started walking. I passed a house where probably a hundred teens and young adults were partying up a storm. Total chaos. I thought drinking would fuel me with liquid courage and help me follow through on my goal of killing myself.

I got drunk quickly and got into an argument with this belligerent A-hole. We started tussling. I wrapped my left arm around this dude's neck and pummeled him with my right hand. I was getting the better of it when—

—the dude reached for a fixed-blade knife inside a sheath on his belt. In a flash, I immediately recognized the Rambo-like knife, but I reacted too late: he stabbed me five times on the left side of my body, in my abdomen.

I fell over and hit the ground, barely conscious. I remember cops arresting the guy and paramedics working on me, but life was leaving my body. I felt death come upon me.

This thought flashed through my mind: *God, I will never know You.* I was resigned to my fate, but there was still a ray of hope. I said to myself, *God, I need you. I need You.*

The next thing I knew, I was floating at the top of the ceiling, looking down at a pair of paramedics administering CPR. Then it was like someone took the ceiling away, and I was moving further into sheer black darkness.

As I turned toward the darkness, away from the picture of my life, I didn't know where I was at all. I heard a voice say, "He's mine. I've been waiting for him."

The voice sounded so evil that I knew Satan was speaking. I was wondering what would happen next when I heard another voice say,

133

"I'm will not let Franko leave Earth without seeing how good he can be. Let him be a testament to Me."

At that moment, I came back into my body. When I opened my eyes, a paramedic was performing chest compressions while two other paramedics were packing up their gear.

"I got a heartbeat!" the paramedic yelled to his colleagues.

That's when I knew I would not die.

Various machines were brought out, and a trio of paramedics started working on me. When they put me on a stretcher for transport, for the first time in my life, I cared about something bigger than me—living.

✦ ✦ ✦

If you're expecting me to say that after I recovered from my near-death experience, known as an NDE, and got on my knees and got right with God, that didn't happen.

For the next five years, I was still the same bad person. I was in and out of prison four times. I got into a relationship and fathered a daughter named Breana.

I phoned the mother on the day I was released from Tehachapi State Prison at twenty-four. I wanted to see how my daughter was doing.

"Hey, I found Jesus," she said. "You want to go to church with me?"

One day, I was in prison; the next day, I was in church.

I took my first step toward the Lord that day, but it wasn't until a godly man named Les Pearsey came into my life that I totally sold out to Christ and put my past behind me.

I joined a Journey discipleship class that Les led in Bakersfield. As he got to know me and heard my story, he said to me one day, "Can I mentor you?"

I didn't know what a mentor was and told him so.

"A mentor is somebody who comes alongside you. He is there for you," he explained.

"Great, let's do it," I replied.

For the next seven years, Les met with me every week, pouring into my life and keeping me on track. I started sharing my story to encourage others, as Casey has done.[2]

I'll end by sharing a story about when I spoke to a church with a homeless outreach on a weeknight. People experiencing homelessness would line up for a free meal, and then I'd be the after-dinner speaker. This happened a few years ago.

I related much the same story as I have here. I couldn't help but notice a young family in the front reaching for hankies and dabbing their eyes.

When I finished, the family approached me.

"You mentioned eating those chili dogs at the 7-Eleven on Wilson and Stine Road," the father said. "That's where our Aunt Ronnie worked."

I knew exactly who he was talking about.

"You mean—"

"Yup," the young father replied. "She told us about this teenage boy who ate from the dumpster for two years. Do you know what she told us?"

"No, I don't."

"She said she prayed every day over that food. She prayed that God's hand would be on your life."

I shivered with emotion. Sure, I'd gotten to know Ronnie long ago and wondered whatever happened to her. "Can I meet her?"

"She just died, but she always influenced us to attend church. That's why we're here today. We wouldn't be here if it weren't for her."

I could say the same for me.

---

2 To fill in the blanks, like Raz, I started my own construction and remodeling company and am no longer "No Show Franko." I've been married more than twenty years to Misty and am the stepfather to her two sons from a previous marriage.

chapter ten

REACHING OUT
IN SALT LAKE CITY

by Heather Anderson *and* Casey Diaz

HEATHER ANDERSON

I work with gang-involved youth in the greater Salt Lake City area and have been involved in gang-affiliated programs and outreaches across several states since 2017.[1]

I'm always looking for new resources to use with the youth I work with. A few years ago, I found a podcast called "Understanding Gangs" that examines street and prison gang structure from the perspective of law enforcement, academics, and former gang members. The latter group is why they invited Casey Diaz to be on the podcast in July 2021.

For one hour and thirty-six minutes, I was deeply moved by Casey's story because I work with kids who are either in gangs or being pressured

---

1 Heather Anderson is not my real name for confidentiality reasons.

to join a clique. I've seen some hard things go down and have lost some kids. I think sometimes when you're working with youngsters that the rest of the world is not aware of or empathetic towards . . . well, it's easy to get discouraged. There are few resources and few believers in my field, so coming across someone like Casey, whose life was radically transformed by God, was incredibly encouraging.

Since the podcast impacted me deeply, I bought a copy of *The Shot Caller*. Once again, I was enthralled. When I finished the book, I took the copy to work with me, figuring that if I could get one of my teenagers to read it, perhaps one more life could be changed as well.

When the new school year started in September 2021, I was assigned to work with a sixteen-year-old whom I'll call Angel. He'd gotten into a gang-involved fight at school when he and four other dudes jumped another kid, so he was labeled as a troublemaker.

After he was referred to me, we sat in my office at this particular high school in the Salt Lake City area. Before my appointment, I prayed and asked the Lord to show me His purpose and intentions, something I do with new kids I'm assigned to. My goal was to help this teenager get on the right track.

While we chatted that first time, Angel shared his heartbreaking backstory that included being estranged from his father. *You really need a dad*, I thought.

That's when I felt led to pick up the copy of *The Shot Caller* that I brought to work. I handed the book to Angel.

"I want you to read this story as if the man who wrote it is talking to you," I said. "Then you can tell me if you like it."

From his file, I knew Angel was not a strong reader. Fifth-grade level at best. "Give it a try," I said with the most encouraging voice I could share.

"I will. Promise."

He started reading *The Shot Caller* during his lunch period. The following day, he dropped by my office, practically beaming.

"I read six pages," he announced.

"Well, good for you," I gushed.

Then I had an idea: talk to his reading teacher. Because of his poor reading skills, Angel was placed in a special class for kids way behind in their reading ability and comprehension. I asked the teacher if Angel could get school credit for reading *The Shot Caller*. Keep in mind that I work in the public school system, and Casey didn't hold back on how Christ changed his life.

"No problem," his teacher said.

Angel gave me progress reports like a play-by-play announcer: *Casey just joined Rockwood . . . yo, he used a screwdriver! . . . Casey just got arrested . . . now he's out of solitary and with the general prison population . . . you can't believe the beatings he took . . .*

Then, six months later, I received the best news ever: "I finished *The Shot Caller*," he said. "It's the first book I've ever read."[2]

I knew this was a cause for celebration at just the right time. I was also aware that a particular gang had Angel in their sights.

"They know where I live," he confided to me. "They know where my little sisters go to school. I don't want to be a target, but I am."

Street pressure, they call it.

A wild thought came to mind: *Let's talk to Casey. See what he has to say.*

Angel was excited by my idea, so I reached out to Casey through his Instagram page in the fall of 2022. To my pleasant surprise, he responded. I told him what was happening—just as I've shared here. We came up with a plan to help Angel.

The next time Angel came to my office, he was sad because of the heavy pressure on his shoulders.

"Let me do something."

---

2 I've since probably purchased twenty copies of *The Shot Caller* and handed them to kids I work with. The impact is always powerful.

"Sure."

I reached for my phone and texted Casey.

Are you free now?

Sure am was the response.

We're ready, I texted back.

When I got a thumbs up, I turned to Angel.

"I have a surprise for you."

"What's that?"

"We're going to get a phone call in a few seconds."

"From—?"

"Casey Diaz."

His whole face lit up. Then a frantic look. "But you haven't given me time to prepare," he moaned. "What am I going to say?"

I was assuring him that everything would be fine when Casey buzzed in on my phone. I put the smartphone on speaker and gave Casey a brief description of his situation—the recruitment from a local gang, the hassles he was receiving.

Casey, who has a unique sixth sense for reading situations and people, had an excellent exchange with Angel. It was one thing for me—a white woman in her early thirties who was called "Blondie" by her first gang kiddo—to say how dangerous it was to adopt the gang lifestyle and quite another when similar thoughts came from Casey, who can sound like the Voice of God when speaking to kids about gang life.

Casey walked Angel through some solid practical advice and then prayed with him on the phone, which was sweet of him to do and meant a lot to my student.

Throughout the rest of the school year, Angel said no to the recruitment, stayed off Instagram for a while, cut off certain friends and groups, and then switched schools to escape the gang drama.

I kept meeting with Angel, who wanted to graduate early so that he could get on with life. I was glad to see him thinking that way.

But one time, he looked at me. "I would really like to meet Casey in person," he said. "Can we invite him to come here?"

In my mind, I was thinking: *There's no way Casey can come to Salt Lake City, but I love that kids like Angel believe that I can make anything happen.*

"Let's see what Casey says," I responded. "Perhaps we could get a group together for him to meet with."

I contacted Casey again and asked if we could figure out a way to fly him out to Salt Lake City and speak to a bunch of good-hearted kids feeling the pressure to join a gang.

Casey said he'd think about it.

CASEY

I thought about it, all right. I was getting a lot of requests to come here and go there. While I took none for granted, I had more speaking and appearance requests than I could handle if I spoke every day for the next year.

There was another dynamic in play: after *The Shot Caller's* release, speaking requests piled in from various prison ministries and gang prevention programs like the one Heather was working with. While I've done plenty of prison ministry and spoken to troubled youth over the years, I was happiest when I got up in front of large men's groups or church congregations. That was feeling like a better fit for me.

Around the time Heather reached out to me, I was networking with Ken McKenzie, the president and CEO of Lean on Me USA, a do-good organization providing hope, guidance, and encouragement to at-risk youth and families of inmates in a nationwide effort to reduce recidivism. They were based in West Palm Beach, Florida.

Ken, white and in his mid-seventies, had more energy than dudes half his age. He was a retired FBI agent—bank robberies were his specialty—who had excellent organization skills and was armed with a "let's think big" attitude. When I told him that I'd been asked to speak before a large group of troubled youth in Salt Lake City, his active mind went wild and crazy.

Let's make this really big, he said. *I can bring Gus Rodriguez with me, and we'll get a film crew to record everything and make a documentary. Prisoners and kids need to see this!*

Woah. Slow down, buddy.

Gus Rodriguez was involved in prison ministry in Miami and someone I'd heard about. I knew Ken hosted a podcast called "Death or Prison" that prisoners could listen to on specially made computer tablets being handed out in various prisons. Prisoners couldn't surf the internet with these tablets, but they could listen to religious podcasts like "Death or Prison" or read Christian-based material, which is where Lean on Me USA came in. Ken said the tablets' content could reach millions of prisoners, so making a documentary would provide great content for this outreach. As usual, Ken was thinking big.

When I mentioned that flying us to Salt Lake City, hiring a local film crew, and paying for hotel rooms and meals cost money, Ken said he could come up with the funding somehow.

When I called Heather about this new development, she was open to the idea of making this event bigger than just me, but having a film crew was a non-starter because of privacy issues. She preferred something more low-key. Heather also reminded me that anything we put together had to be approved by higher-ups, which would be challenging for several reasons:

+ A "gang summit" like this had never been attempted in the Salt Lake City area.

+ The event could be viewed as "too religious" since we were all Christians. I always share the gospel in these types of settings. The fact that this event would happen in Mormon Country was also problematic.

+ Some of the decision-makers above Heather weren't
  Christians.

+ Heather didn't have any budget to defray my travel
  expenses.

But Ken was saying he could raise the money and urged me to bring along another ex-con to share his testimony. "Do you have anybody from your gang that maybe you discipled?" he wondered.

"I do have a guy," I replied. "His name is Hector Prieto. We were in different cliques, but he was in the same gang as me. I didn't meet him until after we both got out, but he's been part of my Bible Study group for the last eight or nine years. I think he'd love to come."

"Great. I'll pay for his flight and hook him up with a room. You, too."

"Really?"

"I'll find sponsors or something."

We talked through what this "gang summit" would look like, which happened in bits and spurts over six months. Meanwhile, Ken said he was working on it. As part of prepping for the trip, he wanted to know everything there was to know about gangs in the Salt Lake City area: how many people were standing on street corners, how much graffiti was on buildings, who were the biggest taggers, how many people had pit bulls, etc.

One time, I teased Ken about his nerdy requests. "You know this isn't Compton, right? We're talking about Utah."

"I know, I know . . ." he replied.

HEATHER

Ken wanted me to bring every gang rival I could find and get them to show up at the venue, where they would presumably be gobsmacked for Jesus by Casey, Gus, and Hector.

I pointed out that if we were going to pull off a "gang summit," we needed armed security, which was always going to be problematic since we'd have to find plainclothes cops the youths didn't recognize.

After a few months of back and forth, cooler heads prevailed. The event was scaled back to something more manageable—we'd invite fifteen kids or so who were *not* part of rival gangs or weren't gang members yet. The invitees would be kids who were okay with each other and wouldn't necessarily cause an issue.

We scheduled the event for Friday, September 22, 2023. The venue would be a mothballed Salt Lake City fire station set for demolition sometime in the future that our organization had refurbished into a "hang-out" place for youth in the area. We had furnished it with a couple of pool tables, a Foosball table, a Ping Pong table, couches, and a big screen TV in the bay where the fire trucks used to be parked. The fire station was viewed as "neutral territory" in the neighborhood, another plus.

It wasn't until August that I received permission to proceed. I figured that only Casey would fly out since we had scaled back things, but Ken was still thinking big. He wanted to still come and bring Gus Rodriguez with him, so I didn't see the harm in that as long as they paid their own way.

As for Casey's travel expenses—he agreed to speak for free—I had a difficult decision to make. The only way I received permission to bring Casey in was if this event didn't cost my agency any money. Then Ken called and said he could cover his flight, hotels, and rental car expenses—but not Casey or Hector's.

Like I said, I didn't have any money to fly in Casey and Hector, so I prayed about what to do. Without Casey, why go forward? Do we cancel? Try another time? The answer I received from the Lord was this: *You pay for everything.*

Talk about taking a leap of faith. I was a single woman living in a small one-bedroom apartment with two cats named Chaos and

Compton. I work for a non-profit and receive a modest salary.

The good news is that the plane tickets on Delta weren't that much. I went for it and booked them.

That's how much I wanted to help young people like Angel. I wasn't going to pull out. I mean, I've lost too many kids to the streets. I didn't know how much time I'd have with each of them. Their souls mattered to me more than anything else. As far as I was concerned, this was worth it.

CASEY

I had no idea Heather paid for the plane tickets for me and Hector until we wrote this chapter. I'm blown away.

HEATHER

Here's the rest of the story. When I got to know Casey in 2022, I was new to Utah. I'd only been here for a year. Let's be honest: in a state where the Mormon religion is predominant, there weren't evangelical Christian churches on every street corner. I was having a problem finding a church home.

So, when Ken was dreaming big, he wanted to get a local church involved.

One of his ideas was to pair each at-risk youth with a mentor after the event. I didn't like the idea because those programs generally don't work. I wasn't interested in putting children whom I love dearly with well-meaning church people who had no idea what they were doing in mentoring at-risk youth.

During one of our phone calls early in our process, Ken said, "I know this pastor at a church in Salt Lake City, so I called him to see if I could get him to help out."

Oh, Lord, help me out of this one. "What's the name of the church?" I asked.

When he told me, I Googled this church as fast as I could while Ken was talking. I discovered this church wasn't very far from my home.

"How about I check out the church first and make sure it's solid," I suggested. I didn't want any bad theology mixed in.

"Sure, go ahead," Ken said. "The pastor said he wanted to meet the person coordinating this event, and that's you."

I showed up the following Sunday morning to see for myself what this church was all about. I liked the worship service and the pastor's preaching. The people were welcoming.

I sat toward the back and prayed, *Lord, I don't know what You're doing, but I know You're behind this somehow, so show me what You want out of this situation.*

After the service, I introduced myself to the pastor.

"Did you receive a phone call this week from somebody named Ken?" I asked.

"Yeah, I did. It was interesting," the pastor said. As we chatted, I definitely got the vibe that he didn't know who Ken was before they spoke on the phone.

The pastor chuckled. "Then he started drilling me with questions, like how many former felons we had in our congregation."

Sounds like dear ol' Ken.

I could tell the pastor didn't know what to do with me since he said, "Well, you're not who I was expecting!" After a few minutes of chitchat, he made eye contact with one of the ladies in the church and passed me off to her.

She was very friendly, asked questions about me and what I did, that sort of thing. She inquired if I was interested in joining a Bible study, and I said sure. I started showing up and getting to know some people at church, including one of the elders and his wife. Again, everyone was very nice, and I felt like I was becoming part of a community of believers.

One evening, the elder asked me if I was the one who was working with gangs. When I said yes, he mentioned that the pastor had told him about our plans to have an outreach event for at-risk youth.

"How can our church get involved?" he asked.

"Actually, there's nothing you can do right now," I responded. This was during the summer of 2023, and we didn't have approval yet. "But if something comes up down the road, I'll let you know," I promised.

I liked my small group and our church, an Acts 29 church plant that had been around for ten years. During the summer, I became a member and finally felt I'd found a church home. I remember thinking, with wry amusement, that only the Lord would use a former FBI member and a former gang member to point me in the direction of a church.

Meanwhile, August came around. I knew plane tickets had to be purchased and reservations made for a rental car and a local hotel. That's when I learned that Ken and Gus were set to go, but I didn't have any budget for Casey and Hector's flights *or* their hotel. I knew we couldn't cancel the event, so I put their plane tickets and hotel reservations on my credit card. I was all in.

Two days before the event, I received a phone call from the elder, who said he'd heard about what I did. (To this day, I don't know how he found out.)

"We support what you're doing," he said. "I want you to send me all the receipts. We can support this as a church, and we want to love on our community in this way and love on you, so we're going to cover it."

He offered to pray for me and the event, which was a blessing. His offer to cover Casey and Hector's expenses confirmed to me that the Lord was behind what we were trying to do.

The day before the event, Casey and Hector flew in from the West Coast, and Ken and Gus arrived from Florida, landing within ninety minutes of each other. I drove out to the Salt Lake City airport to greet them, which was a madhouse because the FanX Salt Lake Comic Convention—a Comic Con-like event—was happening simultaneously.

Hugs were exchanged at the baggage claim when all four men

arrived. I followed Casey and the guys to the rental car line, which was a mess because of the overflow crowds. After an hour in line, they were handed the keys to a car that was nowhere to be found.

"Someone must have stolen it," Casey quipped.

The agency eventually found them another car. I gave the guys directions to my place, where I had invited several church friends to join us. I stayed in my lane for meal prep and cooked pasta with a meat sauce, served with a Caesar salad and parmesan bread.

It was awesome hearing everybody's stories. I knew Casey's, of course, but I didn't know anything about Gus or Hector. We all chuckled when Hector described his first date after being released from prison. He prepared a "prison spread" in which the main ingredient was Ramen instant noodles mixed with whatever he had in the refrigerator—refried beans, sausages, peppers, and the like. "Hey, I didn't know anything different," he said with palms up.

We had a season of prayer that evening, and then they returned to their hotel.

In the morning, I wanted our guests to have the full Utah experience, which meant me picking up some pick-me-up drinks at a Swig soft drink shop, home of the "dirty soda." The Mormon Church prohibits drinking hot caffeinated drinks like coffee or tea, but caffeine in cold beverages is okay. Hence, the rise of soda shops that serve Coca-Cola or Dr Pepper mixed with cherry or vanilla syrup, sweet cream, coconut syrup, lime juice—the list is endless. I showed up at their hotel with a "dirty soda" for all of them, which they loved.

The kids were scheduled to arrive after 3 p.m., but then we got thrown a curveball. Two teen boys—one a gang member, the other a wannabe—wanted to meet Casey, but the gang member was a rival of a bigger clique. I asked them to show up two hours before everyone else arrived to keep them separated. No reason to tempt fate.

And then a second curve ball. Actually, a fastball to the head. I had specifically asked for security for our "summit." I wanted a couple of plainclothes cops or SROs.[3] When the two teens arrived in the early afternoon, we had no security.

Some wires got crossed. We wouldn't see any security that day at all.

CASEY

When we sat down with these two guys, I saw that these kids were very much drawn to Hector and Gus. When I see something working like this, I gladly retreat to the background to not interrupt the developing rapport. I noticed they were hanging on to every word from Hector—and in no hurry to leave as the hour approached three o'clock when the main group would start arriving.

HEATHER

And that's when Angel and some of his friends showed up. I'd say there had been a year-and-a-half worth of drama among these boys with multiple fights.

CASEY

I was playing Ping Pong with one of Heather's staff members after she challenged me to a game. We were going at it when I noticed Angel and his friends come through the front entrance. He looked uneasy to me as his eyes darted from side to side. I thought he was wearing a mask and trying to act cool, but my street smarts told me something was up.

HEATHER

Something was up. I could see it in the glares between the two camps. I stealthily moved and steered Angel toward Casey, where I quickly

---

3 SROs, or school resource officers, are sworn law enforcement officers responsible for safety and crime prevention in schools—and stopping active shooter events.

introduced them and excused myself.

I put my body between the two groups of boys warily approaching the new group of teens. I faced the two boys who had arrived early.

"Guys, you need to leave. It's time to go," I said sternly in my "adult" voice.

They looked at each other. They were respectful of me in my space. One said, "Okay."

I escorted them out the front door. Once outside the firehouse, I ordered an Uber car for them and breathed a sigh of relief. Everything was going to be okay.

We were waiting on the sidewalk for the Uber car to arrive when I heard the door open behind me. To my horror, Angel flew out of the firehouse like his hair was on fire, yelling at the pair, "Come back here! We're going to settle this right now!" Stuff like that.

One of Angel's buddies had followed and tried to restrain him. "Not here, bro," he said. "This is not okay."

But Angel kept coming our way, so it was up to me to step between him and the two boys. "Please, if you have any respect for me, you have to get back into that building, Angel. Like now."

Angel thought a moment, then relented. He allowed his buddy to escort him back to the building.

I turned to the two boys. I felt like I had de-escalated the situation when someone else popped his head out of the firehouse and yelled something at us. The spark was lit all over again, especially for one who was a gang member. I'll call him Juan.

Juan has been involved with a gang all his life, practically born into it since it was generational. Deep roots. Street cred in spades.

I knew that if he lost his temper, it would be impossible to get him under control again. He felt disrespected, and his temper was about to explode. And he thought it was my fault.

"This is on you because you brought me here and is happening on your watch!" he stormed.

My boss had shown up and was inside the firehouse. She called me. "Angel's all upset," she said. "What's happening out there?"

"We're still waiting for the Uber."

"If it doesn't come soon, you have to put them in your car and drive them home," she said. "This is threatening to escalate out of control. If those boys are not out of here in the next minute, I have no alternative but to call the cops."

Those words stung, but she was right. We had girls and younger children in the firehouse. Anything could happen.

Then, the gang member stepped away and reached for his phone. I overheard him call a homie and tell him where to go. *Oh, no. He's calling for backup.*

I knew what that meant. I stepped closer and tried to warn him. "This is out of my hands now," I said firmly. "You have to leave. I just spoke with my boss. She will call the cops if you don't get out of here pronto."

Just then, the Uber car pulled up. Just in time. I exhaled a long breath.

The two boys refused to get into the Uber, however, a move that ticked off the driver. They started cussing out each other, which raised the temperature. Then the Uber driver hopped back in the car, slammed the gear shifter into drive, and sped off with an empty backseat bench.

The situation couldn't worsen, but it did. Another group of boys arrived. They were teen sons of several of my co-workers and had heard that Casey was coming to town. I was glad they came, but nobody had told me they were showing up.

I shoo-shooed them toward the front entrance before they engaged the two boys and escorted them into the building. That's when my boss came up to me.

"I just called the gang unit," she said.

I knew what it meant: if the boys were still out front, they would get arrested, cuffed, and taken to the country jail, where they would be detained until their parents picked them up.

Meanwhile, it was time to start our presentation for the three dozen or so young people we had inside the firehouse. After Ken said a few words, Gus stood up to give his presentation. I checked what was happening outside to see if the gang unit had arrived. Not yet, but then another car pulled up to the sidewalk. I didn't recognize the strange vehicle or the driver and his passenger.

CASEY

Heather didn't tell me there were a couple of homies outside looking to make trouble. But I could tell that Heather was upset for some reason.

Then Heather found me. "We have a situation, and we need to pray," she said.

"Let's do it," I said.

While Gus was speaking, I found Hector and Ken and led them to a small office, where I explained the situation. The four of us gathered in a circle and prayed for everyone's safety and that the young people would have open ears to hear what we had to say.

HEATHER

I was unaware that after the event started, a Salt Lake City police car rolled in. They directed the occupants of the mystery car to step out to be questioned. Nor was I aware that a police search of the mystery vehicle would turn up a gun.

The only good news was that the tall, floor-to-ceiling garage doors had only several small "slit" windows to look outside, so none of the kids knew what was going on, nor me.

That was a good thing. But then I spotted a couple of teen boys looking through another window slit, their eyes getting bigger by the second.

I intercepted them and asked them to step away from the tall garage door. That's when I spotted the SLCPD black-and-white outside.

"I'm going to ask you guys to do something for me right now," I told the boys. "I need you to not tell anybody in this room about what is happening out front. Can you keep that quiet for me?"

They did me a solid and didn't tell anyone.

CASEY

After Hector shared his testimony as an LA gangbanger before God got a hold of him, it was my turn. Batting cleanup.

I was a little more graphic in my talk than I usually am, but I felt the Holy Spirit was giving me the right words to say. The room was quiet—always a good sign. That meant they were listening hard. After sharing my testimony, I ended my talk by presenting the Gospel and asking anyone in that firehouse if they wanted to get right with God like I did in a jail cell.

"I don't like calling these altar calls," I said. "Nor do I like it when preachers ask you to close your eyes and nobody's looking, and then you raise your hand and say this cute little prayer, then you're good to go with God. Because if you start in shame, you'll end in shame. When you become a Christian, you should be bold and let everybody know where you stand."

No sooner had I uttered those words when a little girl, probably no more than ten, stepped forward and stood before me, her eyes searching mine. Two, three girls followed her. And then Angel was the first boy! His boldness opened the floodgates because nearly all the other boys followed him. At least thirty of the three dozen young people in that firehouse came forward to ask Jesus into their hearts and know they would have eternal life with Him.

HEATHER

I know why Angel was the first boy to respond. Before Casey spoke, I noticed Angel sitting in the back, head down, and a hoodie covering him up. I knew him well enough to realize that he was struggling.

I took a seat next to him and touched him on the shoulder.

"Hey, I want you to look at me," I whispered.

He didn't move.

"I need you to look me in the eyes."

When he glanced my way with sad eyes—no doubt because of the way he flew off the handle earlier—I spoke in a low voice. "I need you to take a deep breath and look around this room," I said matter-of-factly.

And he did.

"Every single person is here because of you," I said. "That's right. Because you read a book and followed through and wanted this to happen, look at what's happening here today. You need to recognize that you have had a huge role in this."

I knew Angel had been downplayed his whole life. He had seen a lot in sixteen years. Kids his age get shot. Guys die in the street in front of him. He'd struggled mightily. But he was still here.

He turned to me. "Okay," he said, his way of acknowledging my words.

That's not all that happened when Casey came to Salt Lake City, which showed me that sometimes things don't go the way I plan them, but all God was calling me to do was to be faithful.

Angel turned from an F student to getting As and graduated early from high school, staying out of gangs the entire time. He's the entrepreneurial type, so the hustle continues.

As for Casey, I'd love to have him come back to Salt Lake City anytime. I'm not sure I could survive another evening with Ken, though.

Too many questions and ideas!

chapter eleven

AN ECUMENICAL VISIT

by Rev. Phillip Kaim

Pastor of Holy Family Catholic Church in Rockford, Illinois

Since my middle school days of delivering newspapers before sunrise, I've always been an early riser. The only change is that my wake-up time has gotten earlier over the years.

Now my day begins at 2:20 a.m. when—after some bedside prayers—I spend an hour in prayer before Our Lord in a little chapel inside my rectory home. When I'm done, usually around 3:30 in the morning, I grab my gym bag and head across the street to Anytime Fitness, which, as the name suggests, is open for night owls and early birds like me.

After warming up on an elliptical machine, I spend an hour or so on the treadmill with my iPad, swiping my way through a Kindle version of a book on my reading list. I know some are puzzled at how one can read while walking. I can't entirely explain it, but it sure beats the alternative. Walking on a treadmill would be dreadful without something productive and fruitful to pass the time.

Nearly everything I pore through on my iPad is faith-related, but I try to read different books within the broad topic of faith and religion, which is where *The Shot Caller* fits in.

How did Casey's book make it on my reading list? I'm not entirely sure. Something led me to him. Or should I say Somebody? I have no doubt the Lord is guiding my choices for what I should be putting between my ears.

Like anyone else deciding what to read, I hop on Amazon and check out several reviews about a book before deciding if it would make my list. That's what I did with *The Shot Caller*. What appealed to me was that Casey's book appeared to be a story about how God intervened dramatically in a gang member's life. With a festering gang problem in Rockford, I felt I owed myself to check out Casey's story and see how it might help me better understand a part of our culture that I was mostly ignorant of and would help me in my ministry.

I made a good choice: *The Shot Caller* was so compelling that I didn't want the book to end. What left an indelible impression on me was how much it cost Casey to evangelize other prisoners when he was locked up at New Folsom State Prison. The beatings he took. The wounds he endured. The dangers he faced each time his prison door opened.

Casey's riveting account convinced me that this would be a great story to share with my parishioners at Holy Family—and have Casey do that in person.

✦　✦　✦

Like most churches, getting everyone back to church after the Covid-19 pandemic has been a challenge. We've had some success at Holy Family, but not enough, so I began pouring over parish renewal books, both Catholic and Protestant, to learn what we could do to not only bring some of those people back but bring others to the Lord who did not have God in their lives.

Perhaps the most profound "a-ha" moment came when one of the authors said that your church must put together a conscious effort to make disciples.

Then the author asked these questions:

- ✦ What is your pathway to discipleship?
- ✦ Can you clearly articulate it?
- ✦ Does everyone in the pews know what that pathway is?

Regarding the last question, I realized that if there wasn't a conscious effort to replace the leaders who were running your parish programs, then all the activity going on at a busy parish might collapse in ten years when the people running those programs burn out, move away, or die.

That profound thought resonated with me because we have a lot going on at Holy Family if one goes by the church calendar of events or the rooms booked on any given night. But when I looked at those running those programs, I didn't see a lot of new blood or a healthy turnover in leaders who ran them. *What will it be like ten years from now?* That was one of the questions that kept me up at night.

This explains why, coming out of Covid in September 2022, we launched an extensive evangelism effort that involved multiple programs that would reset the culture of parish life by emphasizing a new pathway to discipleship that my Evangelization Committee and I came up with.

The Discipleship Pathway consisted of four steps:

- ✦ Explore God
- ✦ Encounter Him
- ✦ Expand in Faith
- ✦ Embark on a Mission

I told our congregation that we Catholics weren't very good at the first and last step on that pathway. The first step, *Explore God*, was about creating what we call "entrance ramps" for those who had been away from church or had no experience going to church. A twelve-week Bible study on the book of Revelation wouldn't be a good first step for those returning to church. A better approach might be watching the popular *The Chosen* film series together.

The second step, *Encounter God*, referred to the retreats we offer. I mentioned to my congregation that one can encounter God any-where—in the supermarket talking to someone at the check-out line, going on a nature walk, etc. Still, there's no substitute for the con-centrated, dedicated time a weekend retreat offers. That is very often where we encounter God in a deep and personal way and even make life-altering decisions.

The third step, *Expand in Faith*, was one we were most familiar with. This included the various Bible and book studies that are a staple of most Christian churches.

But it was the last step on this pathway—*Embank on a Mission*—that we weren't doing well. We often get excited about something we have just experienced at church, but we don't take the next step and share what we experienced with others. That's what we had to get better at and where Casey came in because what struck me most about him was his passion for evangelization, which leaped off the pages.

We are an Incarnational church—"the Word became flesh and dwelt among us." Everything becomes more real to us when we see it in the flesh. I knew it would not have the same effect if I told my congregation to read his book. They needed to see Casey's passion for sharing the love of God in person. If that happened, I was confident some of his passion would rub off on them.

Before I invited Casey to Holy Family, though, I considered the theological differences between his evangelical Christianity and our Catholic beliefs. I don't downplay those differences. They are real. But

I think with Casey's story, we can appreciate how much a heart can change from a life of violence and crime to a life of faith and hope, regardless of our faith differences. Any Christian can be inspired by what God has done in Casey's life and his passion for sharing Jesus with others, even if we may not hold to all the same theological tenets.

Even though I had never asked a non-Catholic to make a significant address to our congregation, I knew Casey's story of redemption inside New Folsom and his bravery when telling other gang members that he would no longer be a gang member would inspire every parishioner, young and old.

I found his website at caseydiaz.net and used the Contact form. It wasn't long before Casey and I spoke on the phone. I immediately liked him and quickly established a rapport.

"Have you ever spoken in a Catholic church?" I asked.

"No," replied, "but I've done a few Catholic podcasts and was interviewed on the Catholic cable station, EWTN. You'd be the first."

That was good enough for me. "Would you like to come out from Los Angeles to share your story?" I asked.

"Of course," Casey replied.

We made the necessary arrangements, and I thought it would be good for Casey to meet some Catholics, visit with our schoolchildren, and learn a little bit about our faith. I intended to budget some time to give him some basics about our Catholic faith and some resources he could consult.

✦ ✦ ✦

I volunteered myself to pick up Casey at Chicago's O'Hare Airport, a bit more than an hour southeast of Rockford.

After some get-to-know-you talk, I asked Casey why he didn't mention how many beatings he received in prison in *The Shot Caller*.

"You're a sharp reader," Casey said, "because a lot of people don't pick up on that. But I stopped counting at twenty-seven."

This part of Casey's story may have been what I was most touched and impressed by. That Casey—in total obscurity inside the prison walls—would take those kinds of beatings and offer that kind of sacrificial love was heart-warming, even though he knew that the next pummeling might be the last one. He could very well have died from those beatings, and no one would have ever known why or about God's intervention in a dramatic way in his life. But he accepted those beatings anyway.

Nor did he choose to "rat out" the gang members who were knocking him around with their fists and kicking him with their feet. What a form of evangelization through the witness of his life! In fact, his book described those who were converted *after* seeing him being pounded into a bloody mess. "Something dramatic must be going on," they probably said to themselves, something beyond just a desire to leave gang life.

It would appear that what Casey endured in prison—taking all those blows to the body and turning the other cheek—is what ultimately sprung Casey from prison early. The parole board— "Maximum John" included—realized that the conversion of his heart was profound and real.

During our drive from O'Hare, I asked Casey if he would also speak to all our fifth through eighth graders at our parochial school. There is a growing Hispanic population at Holy Family. About half of all our new students come from Hispanic families, which was another compelling reason for him to speak to our kids.

Casey was enthusiastic about addressing the kids, which he did in the early afternoon at St. Gabriel Hall, our fellowship hall at Holy Family. Although the boys may have wanted to hear the gory details, Casey focused on his conversion experience and how God desired to have a relationship with him, regardless of his past as a former gang leader. The impressionable students understood that we weren't talking about traffic violations here. About one hundred and fifty kids were spellbound by his presentation.

When his talk was over, a dozen older boys asked Casey for his autograph. That's how wowed these youngsters were, which was great to see. Even better, I know some of the kids went home telling their parents, "Mom, Dad, you have to go see Casey tonight!" In other words, the kids evangelized their parents!

Before the evening talk, I spent some time giving Casey some resources about the Catholic faith that addressed some of the common misconceptions people have about Catholicism. I also took him to our Adoration Chapel, open 24/7 for prayer. He was impressed with the foot traffic—people coming in and out, taking a few minutes out of their busy schedule to spend time with Our Lord.

After a quick dinner, it was time for his talk. Perhaps the word-of-mouth buzz is why we had an excellent turnout later that evening at St. Gabriel Hall, where 350 turned up on a Monday evening in October.

One of the things he mentioned that really struck me was how his heart changed instantly when he had that experience of Jesus appearing to him on his prison wall. His heart went from seeing violence as the answer to everything to what we could all see: a humble and gentle soul that radiated the love of Christ. Watching Casey literally weep about the sins he committed while in the gang life filled the congregation with the hope that they too could have God change their hearts. They reasoned that if He could change Casey's heart so dramatically and quickly, then He could change theirs as well.

That evening, as Casey drew things to a close, he turned reflective. Casey then said something that really struck a chord with our parishioners: "Real wealth is when all your children are worshiping Jesus in their adult lives."

He made a strong impression when discussing his family—his marriage to Sana and the three children they've raised. The two oldest are daughters in their early twenties who are quite involved in their faith. One of them is an assistant worship leader at her church.

That said a lot to the Holy Family parents because they know how difficult it is to raise kids in today's culture. We must be intentional about practicing the faith these days because the secular world has so many mechanisms to draw us away from God and the Church. Even sending our children to a Catholic school doesn't mean they won't get caught up in the material world. If our kids go to Harvard and get all these great degrees and make a lot of money but don't have a strong faith in God, then they will experience a form of poverty, a poverty of soul.

When Mother Teresa left the slums of Calcutta and visited the United States, she talked about the poverty of the soul she saw in this "land of plenty." Casey's message to parents about the riches of raising children who take their faith seriously fell on welcome ears in my parish.

His talk ended with a rousing standing ovation. He was a huge hit, and I would recommend Casey to any Christian church, any denomination.

A week after his visit, I reflected on the twenty-seven-plus beatings he took in prison in my newsletter column. I rhetorically asked my readers, "What does that sound like to you?"

Then I answered my own question and said it sounded like the Twelve Apostles, post-Resurrection, to me. The fact that they were willing to take beatings and be martyred for Christ (the exception being the apostle John, who was exiled to the island of Patmos) proved to be an effective evangelization tool. Many conversions occurred in the apostolic age because they knew no one would die for a hoax.

✦ ✦ ✦

After Casey had answered the last inquiry from parishioners who lined up for the chance to ask him a question, he and I, along with my associate, Father Akan Simon, gathered for a photo. Casey, with his passion for evangelization, insisted it be taken in front of the place where we do baptisms.

One of the things we did at Holy Family was to construct a visible reminder of our commitment to evangelism by creating an enormous graphic artwork on a large wall overlooking the church foyer. We framed

Jesus' words from what's commonly called "The Great Commission" found in the twenty-eighth chapter of Matthew so that our parishioners would be reminded of our fourth step on the pathway:

> *"Go therefore and make disciples of all nations, baptizing them in the name of the Father and of the Son and of the Holy Spirit."*

I didn't think this about until recently, but that picture of the three of us represents quite a spectrum of "all nations"—a South Side of Chicago Polish-American, an El Salvadorian immigrant, and a native to Nigeria united in our purpose to make disciples and baptize them in the name of the Father and of the Son and of the Holy Spirit.

You can't get more ecumenical than that.

chapter twelve

A LOOK TO THE FUTURE
by Casey Diaz

As I wound up my talk at Holy Family, I told them that the beatings stopped when the warden shipped out every single Hispanic gang member from our unit to different prisons. My Bible study mate Abel Ruiz and I were the only Latinos to stay behind. I remember inmates from other prisons and county jails filling the empty cells in our pod. None of them had a history with us.

It was like I was starting over with a clean slate. The beatings and persecution stopped. And evangelism began.

Abel and I could speak freely with other inmates. We would send "kites" or notes made from a small piece of yellow paper to share the gospel. In the past, shot callers used kites to order a hit or run drugs, but we used this method of communication to share short, simple messages:

> *God loves you, and He's going to use you. Read 1 John 4:9-10.*

Or this:

> *Let this message encourage you today: It is the Lord who goes before you. He will be with you; He will not leave you, nor will He forsake you. Do not fear or be dismayed.*

These were the same words spoken to me by Frances Proctor, a genteel, older African American woman who visited New Folsom every month when I was locked up in solitary confinement. Time after time, as part of her prison ministry, she came to my gate and said, "I'm praying for you, and I believe God is going to use you."

I'm sorry to say this, but I laughed in her face more times than I know. But she blew on the faint embers of hope that resided deep within my heart until the day Jesus met me in my cell in a miraculous way.

And then another miracle: I got paroled early, and the rest is history.

Look at what the Lord has done and is continuing to do! Sure, sharing my "shot caller" story in a book, on TV with interviewers like Laura Ingraham, and places like Holy Family Catholic Church is nothing short of amazing. Still, it's not the most significant thing that has happened to me since my release nearly thirty years ago. I'm most proud of forming a family with my wife, Sana, and raising three children who love Jesus and are all serving the Lord. That's my greatest treasure, the source of any wealth I have.

One of my daughters, Miah, as Father Kaim mentioned, is the assistant worship director at Arbor Road Church in Lakewood, California. You can go on YouTube and listen to her beautiful voice as she sings "Holy Spirit" with her sister, Samantha, an eighth-grade English teacher. There's nothing better for a father, I can assure you.

Our sixteen-year-old son, Jacob, began a Christian club at his private school that he's been leading for a couple of years. When I was his age, I was leading my homeboys into rival neighborhoods to loot and steal, take part in carjackings, and settle scores in violent ways. But my son is guiding his peers toward a closer relationship with Jesus.

That's what real wealth looks like. It's not money, and it's not having the nicest house on the hill. It's when your sons and daughters love the Lord Jesus Christ and serve Him with all their hearts, minds, and souls. That is wealth they will take into eternity.

God has been so good to me. I have no formal education. I never went to any university except to drop off my kids. I have nothing hanging on my wall that says I earned this degree or passed this course.

What I do have is the joy of the Lord, and there's nothing better. As I go through life, I carry the Psalm 1 in my heart:

> *Blessed is the one*
> *who does not walk in step with the wicked*
> *or stand in the way that sinners take*
> *or sit in the company of mockers,*
> *but whose delight is in the law of the Lord,*
> *and who meditates on his law day and night.*
> *That person is like a tree planted by streams of water,*
> *which yields its fruit in season*
> *and whose leaf does not wither—*
> *whatever they do prospers.*
> *Not so the wicked!*
> *They are like chaff*
> *that the wind blows away.*
> *Therefore the wicked will not stand in the judgment,*
> *nor sinners in the assembly of the righteous.*
> *For the Lord watches over the way of the righteous,*
> *but the way of the wicked leads to destruction.*
> —Psalm 1:1–6 (NIV)

At one time, I was marked for destruction. I've often said that I wouldn't be alive if I hadn't been arrested and sent to prison. But God's grace—and patience—saved me for eternity and allowed me to share the gospel.

That's one reason why the inscription I saw high on the wall at Holy Family church—"Go and make disciples"—meant so much to me. What a great reminder of the importance of going out and telling people about Jesus, about how real He is and how alive He is today.

The Bible says that whoever wins souls is wise (Proverbs 11:30). If you want to keep getting wisdom, tell people about Jesus.

✦ ✦ ✦

Nowadays, winning souls can be done through screen time, like Instagram clips or Facebook posts, or by watching movies on streaming services like Netflix or Amazon Prime or in theaters.

Ever since *The Shot Caller* was released in early April 2019, I started dreaming again about how my book could be turned into an impactful film. Back in Mical Pyeatt's chapter, he told the story of how we had doors slammed in our faces after we commissioned Michael Petrone to write a screenplay and produce a ten-minute trailer. That doesn't mean we gave up. I've long felt that God would open a new door into the filmmaking world and my story would be told in the right way.

Turned out we didn't have to wait long after the release of *The Shot Caller*. Within a few months, Mical and I heard from a handful of production companies who expressed an interest in turning my book into a movie.

As they say in Hollywood, we took a few meetings, leading to several interesting exchanges. I remember telling one producer firmly and directly, "The only way we will work with you is if you agree not to change anything in the story. You can do whatever Hollywood thing you must do here and there. We understand the creativity of that, but you will not call Him the Big Man Upstairs or some Higher Power. You will refer to Him by His name, and His name is Jesus. If you agree to call Him by that name in this movie, then we can keep talking about working together."

The producer heard me. He was cordial enough, but our meeting didn't last much longer, which was okay. Mical and I knew he would change the story and take Jesus out of the film. That was obvious to us after the pitch. Time to move on.

✦ ✦ ✦

In 2020, Andriana Williams, who runs the Inspire division at Zero Gravity Management, a leading film and television production company, was on the FaithGateway website when she came across an excerpt from *The Shot Caller*.[1] She was instantly intrigued and ordered a copy of the book. Upon arrival, she dove into reading my story.

Andriana told her husband, Mark, owner of Zero Gravity, "I really think this is a film project that we can be passionate about." She was moved by my heartbreaking childhood and by everything I went through at New Folsom. She shared with Mark my vivid gang life and my subsequent 180 in solitary.

Mark was skeptical, however. He felt there were already enough prison movies out there.

"This one is different," she responded. "The story goes from the depths of depravity to hope. It shows the evil of Casey's choices but then shifts to reveal his compelling transformation. His change is not some flash in the pan. Thirty years later, Casey is still living as a changed man."

So Andriana tracked me down, and we got on a call. Then, Mical and I trekked to their LA office to meet with her and Mark one morning. We felt like we hit it off from the first handshake and hug.

During our meeting, Mical asked Mark point-blank, "Have you read *The Shot Caller*?"

"No, I haven't," Mark responded.

Mical, who can be a real bulldog on this, was emphatic that Mark

---

1 FaithGateway is where the publisher of *The Shot Caller*, HarperCollins, provides an online community for readers to check out daily blog posts, devotionals, and book excerpts.

needed to experience my remarkable story.

Over the next few weeks, Andriana and Mark went through the book together in the evenings. The words came alive on the page, galvanizing the couple. Andriana asked us to drive out to the office again.

"There are unusual hurdles with this *Shot Caller* project because it's foreign turf," she began. "Other than *The Passion of the Christ*, I'm hard-pressed to think of another R-rated violent film that supports a Christian message. This is a radical departure from what's typical in Hollywood since this project doesn't fit cleanly into any genre. A *Shot Caller* movie would have action-packed grit, heart, wickedness, and faith-based elements—and would likely be rated R. With our newfound hyper-divisive culture, once it's clear your positive transformation is founded in the Christian message, people who aren't of faith may react negatively to the story. Yet showing raw, visceral criminality could likely be off-putting for Christians too," she said.

We all agreed that faith-based films are often criticized for being too saccharine, even by Christians.

"People of faith could be so repelled by the domestic violence and gang life that they may fail to appreciate the beauty of your redemption," she said. "But if we water down the evil, the story could lose the impact of your incredible change. A candle in pitch black seems to glow brighter than when it's in an already lit room. Similarly, we hope the dark juxtaposed against the light can allow the light to shine brighter."

Mical and I listened, taking everything in. Both my world and my decisions had been horrible and depraved, but we knew we did not want to make a fluffy movie that diluted the reality of my life's choices nor the power of God working in my life.

During our meetings, I enjoyed learning about Andriana's background. She is the daughter of missionaries who worked with Greater Europe Mission (GEM). In the field, her father, John, helped found a school of theology in Athens, Greece. After the family moved to British Columbia, her father was a pastor and later got into prison ministries full-time.

"As a little girl, I went to prison on visiting day with my family," she told us. "We'd have meals with the inmates and get to know them. Naively, I remember asking my dad, 'Why do we only have plastic forks and knives in here?'"

We all chuckled when she said that.

"My parents are my heroes for their integrity and the love they show everyone," Andriana continued. "Witnessing my dad's humongous heart, compassion, and wisdom for his work—and seeing inmates' lives change in hugely positive ways—drew me to your story. Putting myself in your shoes, if I were subjected to the unfair suffering that you endured as a kid, I'd have a skewed view of the world too. Convicts often become more corrupt inside the prison system. Yet you emerged from prison a redeemed man because of how God changed you and the work you put in."

Despite recognizing these innate challenges to this out-of-the-box project, Andriana was passionate enough to take it on, as was Mark. Zero Gravity set out to craft a screenplay.

After we made an agreement to work together, challenging events began to happen to Andriana and Mark in an *Ok, I will* kind of way. Every area of their lives was hit like an avalanche of nonstop turmoil.

It started with Andriana breaking a small bone in her foot. Per her doctor's instructions, she had to stay off her feet for six weeks. Next, a pipe burst in their home, which demolished two floors. Massive amounts of water seeped through the upstairs floor, ran down the walls, and made the floor beneath like a swamp. The flood displaced them for sixteen months, costing Mark and Andriana countless hours hunting down materials and working with contractors to make their home livable again.

Shortly after the reconstruction was finally complete, a fire threatened their house when they were out of the country. Neighbors evacuated and sent them videos, reporting that their roof was engulfed in a firestorm. The video footage was shocking; for hours, Mark and Andriana thought their house was burning down. Thirty firetrucks and six helicopters showed up. Firefighters closed off the neighborhood, not allowing any incoming traffic into the area, and swarmed their property.

Thankfully, the footage was deceiving. The reality was this: although the fire started on their property, the flames amazingly traveled *away* from their house. They were extremely grateful their home was spared, but the fire was another stressful event.

On top of all that, a litany of health problems hit their extended family. Andriana's father was hospitalized twice, with doctors reporting that they weren't sure he would make it each time. Then, Andriana suffered a concussion from an accident. Later, she went through massive, rapid hair loss, resulting in losing over 50 percent of her hair.

Andriana had been a hair model in print advertising, but now her thick mane was gone. This affliction, where hair falls out in handfuls, is known as *telogen effluvium* and usually resolves itself. But in her case, the condition triggered a permanent hair loss condition. The doctor put her on medication and told Andriana that she'd have to be on it for the rest of her life. Unfortunately, this drug also came with many unwanted side effects, like chronic insomnia.

These events pale in comparison to other things that transpired that were exceptionally unusual or difficult. In short, every area of her and her husband's lives was hit, causing turmoil and headaches.

"The story of our lives is still being written," Andriana said. "As for *The Shot Caller* movie, we're hoping the world is ready for a story with grit and grace like this. It seems our culture may be primed for relevant, raw, and real stories like Casey's."

She and Mark remain committed to bringing *The Shot Caller* to the screen and have vowed to press on. I believe they can get it done.

✦ ✦ ✦

I don't know when or where the cinematic version of *The Shot Caller* will wind up—as a feature film in your local Cineplex or streaming on a platform like Netflix, Amazon Prime Video, Hulu, HBO Max, Paramount, etc. That's in God's hands.

What I do know is that this journey started when I knelt on a concrete floor in a windowless solitary confinement cell and started confessing my sins.

God, I'm sorry for stabbing so many people.

God, I'm sorry I robbed so many families.

With each new confession, I felt another weight come off my shoulders. When I finished, I knew something significant had happened.

Surrendering my life to Jesus that day was like whispering these words:

Ok, Lord. I will.

chapter thirteen

THE REST OF THE STORY

by Casey Diaz

There's one final anecdote that I want to share, and it comes from a question I often hear when I meet folks who have read *The Shot Caller*:

Whatever happened to your parents?

It's a valid inquiry—and reminds me that I have some sharp readers. After I was sentenced for second-degree murder and armed robbery and caught a chain to New Folsom State Prison, I barely mentioned my parents throughout the rest of my book. I wrote that I received letters from my mother, Rosa, who never visited me at New Folsom, which is just outside of Sacramento. I understood why: the four-hundred-mile drive was too far from Los Angeles, and she needed to keep working.

I didn't have anything else to say about my father, Rommel. He never wrote, never phoned, and, as far as I was concerned, didn't care about me one bit. The feeling was mutual.

So what happened to my parents after I got on with life, married

Sana, and began raising a family with her?

I'll start by referring to Chapter 7 in this book, where my brother, James, described how he and my mother drove to my apartment in San Pedro shortly after my release to meet my best friend at New Folsom, Abel Ruiz. After their arrival, I stepped out to get some chips and soda pop at a nearby convenience store since I had nothing in the fridge or kitchen cabinets to serve them.

Upon my return, you can imagine the emotions I felt when I saw James, my mother, and Abel standing in a circle, hands clasped as Abel led them through the Sinner's Prayer. My mother and my only sibling said yes to Jesus!

It wasn't long after that my mother moved to . . . Alaska. A friend told her that one of the 49th state's largest seafood processors, Peter Pan Seafoods, was looking for people to work the line at King's Cove in the Aleutian Islands, the site of one of their four processing plants. If you could hack the smell of cut-up fish and work in a cold, wet, and noisy environment wearing work gloves, hair nets, earplugs, and heavy rain gear and boots, it was the perfect job for you. Housing and food would be covered; meals would be eaten in a company mess hall.

My mother, who'd always been the adventurous sort, was game. Moving to one of the most remote places in the United States was also a great way, in her mind, to get away from all the commotion with my dad. They weren't living together, but he had a way of dropping by her apartment when he needed something, if you catch my drift.

The season at King's Cove—only accessible by boat or small plane—lasted eight months. My mother would filet cod, whitefish, and salmon six, seven days a week, working herself to the bone, and then send James and me money out of the goodness of her heart. She remained a mother who would do anything for her kids. She was also a soft touch: my mother wired money to cousins or someone from the old neighborhood who needed help, demonstrating her enormous heart.

For seventeen years, my mother traveled to King's Cove and worked the processing line, and then returned to LA at Thanksgiving time to winter in Los Angeles. My mother stayed with her sister, Isabelle, and maintained a relationship with my father.

I didn't want to close the door on my relationship with my father after I got out of prison, especially after Sana and I brought three children into the world during the '00s. I wanted him to know his grandchildren, so I told him to call me anytime he wanted to see us and the kids. Whenever he came to the house, he always arrived with a backpack slung over his shoulder.

I'd ask him the same question each time: "What do you have in the backpack? You don't have alcohol, do you?" Sana and I were of one mind on this topic: there would be no alcohol in our home. No ands, ifs, or buts.

I remember the first time I asked him whether he had alcohol in his backpack. He shot me a look that said, *Yeah, you got me.* It was almost like he wanted to lie, but he couldn't.

"Then leave it outside," I said. "I don't want any liquor in this house."

He left a couple of gold cans of Coors next to the front door and respected our wishes. But we noticed there would be a few times when he drank his beer before he knocked on our front door. Not good. I had to be direct with my father. "You have to be sober when you come here," I said. "I don't want a drunk you. I want a sober you."

His visits were cordial and sometimes poignant. I remember when my son Jacob was a preschooler, riding one of those plastic Big Wheel tricycles around the living room floor. My father and I watched Jacob squeal with delight as he churned his legs and "crashed" into our furniture. Then my dad did the oddest thing: he got on the floor with Jacob and helped him "spin out," which elicited more unbridled joy from my son.

My dad on his hands and knees, playing with Jacob on his Big Wheel? I was taken aback because I never got that from him. But I had to give

177

my father credit: he was attempting to spend quality time with my son. I was cool with that and enjoyed those moments. I also noticed that he was also finding more work. With all the home remodeling going on in the Los Angeles area, he possessed skills that were in high demand. My father was great at smoothing cement pours for new driveways or hanging tile in kitchens and bathrooms. Still, there were too many occasions when his drinking and cocaine use would get the best of him.

This was the father I knew all too well whenever we saw each other. He liked to stir the pot by constantly belittling me with put-downs and sarcastic comments; I chalked up to his wrath and loose tongue from too much liquor or being high on something. Whenever I was on the edge of responding in kind, I'd have to excuse myself and get out of there before I said something I'd regret.

That pretty much sums up what was happening with my parents leading up to the publication of *The Shot Caller* in the spring of 2019.

✦ ✦ ✦

Nine months earlier, in June 2018, my father was walking through MacArthur Park, the neighborhood he lived in near downtown LA. It was daytime, so there was plenty of light. Suddenly, he collapsed, hitting the sidewalk and tumbling into the gutter.

My unconscious dad lay there in the street, not moving.

My father had one thing going for him: he didn't look like a homeless guy who'd fallen on hard times. He always made sure he wore clean clothes and kept himself presentable, which may explain why a Good Samaritan came to his aid and called 911. Paramedics arrived on the scene, stabilized my father, and drove him to a nearby hospital.

My father had left his apartment without his wallet, so there was no ID on his person. Unable to articulate his name or Social Security number, the hospital gave him a John Doe designation. Bottom line: he wasn't going anywhere.

After three weeks in the hospital, the administration staff found a match on his fingerprints: their patient was named Rommel Diaz. This led to someone from the hospital contacting my Aunt Isabelle, who, in turn, phoned my mother in King's Cove, Alaska.

My mother didn't hesitate. Even though it was early summer in Alaska—high season for commercial fishing—she made arrangements to return to Los Angeles as soon as possible to be at my father's bedside. She quit her job to come to my father's aid.

At some point, the hospital released my father, who remained in poor shape but had recovered enough to regain his ability to speak and carry on conversations. He couldn't move around, however, and was confined to his bed in his apartment's single bedroom. Nonetheless, my mother insisted on staying with him and caring for my father, sleeping on the couch each night. She administered meds, changed oxygen tanks, and fed him home-cooked meals. The state of California provided caretakers, so my mother got some help during the day.

I knew none of this was going on, however. That was how our family rolled.

On Thursday afternoon in June, around 3:30 in the afternoon, I received a phone call from my mother. I thought she was calling from Alaska because our conversation started normal in every way when she asked me questions like *How are you doing? How is Sana? How are the kids?* That sort of thing.

I sensed something was off, though. "Are you alright?" I asked. "Everything good?"

There was a hesitation, then a flat, declarative sentence: "Your dad just died."

Just like that, she shared the stunning news.

"What? Wha—?"

"Yeah. Your dad. He just died."

She wasn't crying or anything. I think she was in shock. I was thrown off, too, by the sudden news.

"When did it happen? How did it happen?" I asked.

179

In halting sentences, she explained that she had come down from Alaska to care for my ailing father, who'd collapsed on a sidewalk in MacArthur Park and been rushed to the hospital. She'd been caring for him at his place for the last week or two. In the last day or two, my father had taken a turn for the worse.

"I wish you had called me. Where's he right now?" I was referring to his body.

"He's next to me, in his bed. I'm waiting for the mortuary to show up."

"I'm coming over right now. But let me call Sana and see if she can go with me."

"Okay."

I phoned my wife, but we agreed that since it was rush hour, it would take too long for me to get where she was and then drive us to MacArthur Park. I told her I would go it alone. When I arrived at my father's place, the body was gone.

Now it was my turn to be in shock. "What happened, Mom?"

"The mortuary got here pretty quick."

They sure did. That's when I found out something else I didn't know: my mother had pre-purchased plots and funeral arrangements for me, my brother, our spouses, and my father and herself. I don't know how she did it with the bit of money she made, but she had.

I looked around my father's apartment, which smelled like death. "I don't think it would be a good idea for you to stay here tonight," I ventured. "Why don't you come home with me and stay with us as long as you want until we figure out what to do next."

My mother nodded. "That would be nice," she said.

I drove her back to our Burbank home, and we had a nice evening with my family. Around ten o'clock, Sana and Jacob retired (my daughters were off at college), but my mother and I stayed up, talking.

It was a sweet time, reminiscing about the past and where the Lord had taken us. We were still chatting past midnight when she

THE REST OF THE STORY

said, "Two days ago, I was talking to your dad. I got to really have a heart-to-heart talk with him about, you know, his spiritual condition."

This was interesting to hear. I sat up on my couch and leaned in. "What did you say?"

"I went straight to the heaven-and-hell part, that subject," she replied. "I told him, 'God is giving you a chance now. If you pass away without the Lord, you're going to go to hell forever. God's giving you an opportunity to repent and come to him. Right now.'"

"Did he listen?"

"He was listening. Then I told him, 'I just want you to know I forgive you for everything you've done to me and my sons.' Something broke in him when I said that. Tears came to his eyes. He knew he didn't deserve forgiveness, yet I said I had forgiven him. When I asked him again if he wanted to get right with God, with great emotion, he said yes. So I led him to the Lord, and he prayed with me to receive Him in his heart. I led him through a prayer of repentance. When we said 'Amen,' he was crying again. That's when I knew he had truly repented. Then he said something to me."

"What?" I couldn't believe what I was hearing.

"He said, 'Tell Darwin and James that I'm so sorry for failing them.'"

Hearing him say that was very comforting to me, even after all that he had done to me—the beatings, the verbal abuse, the physical neglect. He hadn't been much of a dad or father, but at the end of the day, I didn't want anybody to go to hell, especially my next of kin. I mean, God doesn't want that either, right? I was authentically happy to know that he was with the Lord, that he wasn't in hell, a place that Jesus said was eternal (Matthew 25:41), physical (Matthew 10:28), and horrifying (Mark 9:43).

"I'm so happy he made that decision for Christ," I said. "I wish I would've known. I would have come over."

"I know you would have."

When I shared this fantastic news with Mical Pyeatt, he said something interesting. "Think about it this way. Your father gets to see Jesus before you do," he said.

His simple statement floored me because he was right. At that moment, my father—who didn't want to hear anything I had to say about Jesus or how my life changed after I gave my heart to Him—was on the Other Side with the Lord of the Universe. He was in heaven, a real place described 276 times in the New Testament alone and explained as a setting where there is no more sin, no more tears, and absolute joy at being one with God our creator.

What happened to my father at the eleventh hour and fifty-ninth minute of his life reminded me of the story Jesus told about the vineyard workers in Matthew 20. In this parable, Jesus declared that the kingdom of heaven was like a landowner who went out early into town to hire workers for his vineyard. They agreed to the wage he offered, which was a denarius, the usual daily wage of a day laborer. To put that amount in today's terms, let's call it $125 for a full day of work, from sunup to sundown.

The landowner had a lot of hoeing and raking needed for his rows of ripening vines, so he went out at 9 a.m. and hired several more hands, saying he would pay them "whatever is right" (Matthew 20:3, NIV). Maybe they had heard that this landowner paid fairly, so they agreed and grabbed shovels and rakes for the day ahead. The landowner did the same thing—hiring more workers at noon, three o'clock, and even five o'clock.

As the sun lowered in the sky, the vineyard owner instructed his foreman to call it a day and pay everyone who worked. Those hired last—at five o'clock—were paid first: they were handed $125 in cash, a lot of money for an easy hour of work. The rest of the crew started grumbling. With anger in their voices, they said, "What about us? We slaved all day under a scorching sun, so aren't we going to get more?"

The landowner replied to the worker speaking for the rest. "Friend,

I haven't been unfair. We agreed on a wage of $125, didn't we? So take it and go. Can't I do what I want with my money? That's why many of the first will end up last, and the last will end first."[1]

My father, who probably started "working" at 5:59 p.m., received the same wage as I will on the Day I meet Him. In God's economy, that's perfectly just and fair, and I must accept that. And I do.

Sana thinks the way God saved my father is a reminder that no matter how hard or how bad someone treats me, God is still interested in that person. I need to extend mercy to those who harmed me like my father did, which I've chosen to do.

Now we come to the close of *Ok, I Will*. Each amazing story shared on these pages should remind you that God orchestrates our steps in ways we often can't see in the moment. What appears to be coincidences do not happen by chance or accident but are part of a larger divine plan choreographed by God.

Let these stories build your faith and inspire hope and encouragement within you.

Perhaps the next time you hear a still voice in your heart or something out of the ordinary happens to you, you'll be prompted to respond to God's guidance, wisdom, and love.

I can assure you there's no better way to go through life.

---

1 The dialogue is inspired by The Message translation for Matthew 20.

ACKNOWLEDGMENTS

from Casey Diaz *and* Mical Pyeatt

We want to acknowledge the people who prayed and encouraged us through this adventure.

But most of all, we want you to know that *Ok, I Will* contains only a small fraction of the amazing stories we've witnessed or heard about. The most important person in this book is Jesus Christ, whose hand has been on everything. We encourage you to seek a relationship with Him. That relationship is real, powerful, and available to anyone, no matter how far down you've fallen.

Ask Him, and you'll see.

ABOUT THE AUTHORS

DARWIN "CASEY" DIAZ is a native of El Salvador and a former gang leader. Growing up on the mean streets of Los Angeles, he was forced to fight for his life. He was eventually incarcerated as one of the most violent criminals in California and placed in solitary confinement.

His life was forever changed in that cell when one day God approached Casey in a miraculous way. Upon his release from prison, Casey learned the sign-making business and started his own signage company. These days, Casey enjoys leading Bible studies, being a part-time pastor at Shepherd Church in Porter Ranch, California, and sharing his story with audiences around the country. Grateful for a second chance at life, Casey has been married to Sana for twenty-five years and is the father of three children: Samantha, Miah, and Jacob.

His website is www.caseydiaz.net.

MIKE YORKEY, who collaborated with Casey Diaz in *The Shot Caller*, is the author or co-author of more than 120 books. In the past, he has worked with:

- Walt Larimore, who shares the heroic story of his father fighting in World War II in *At First Light*
- Elishaba Doerksen, who grew up as the oldest of fifteen children with an abusive father in *Out of the Wilderness*

- ex-NFL wife Cyndy Feasel in *After the Cheering Stops*
- Ron Archer, who was sexually abused as a child in *What Belief Can Do*

Mike is also the co-author of the best-selling *Every Man's Battle* series and two World War II novels, *The Swiss Courier* and *Chasing Mona Lisa*. His website is mikeyorkey.com.

INVITE CASEY
TO SPEAK TODAY

CASEY DIAZ is a humble, thoughtful speaker with a passion for sharing how God can save anyone—including someone like himself after he was convicted of committing gang-related crimes and killing another gang member.

Casey is available to speak in church pulpits, men's and women's weekend conferences, and vacation retreats. If you, your church, or your community organization would like Casey to come speak at your event, contact him through his website at caseydiaz.net or write caseydiaz72@gmail.com.

You can also follow him on social media:

Facebook: Casey Diaz-Author

Instagram: caseydiaz#theshotcallerbook

X (Twitter): caseydiaz#theshotcallerBK